Buddhist Studies Series : 1
General Editor: Prof. S R Bhatt

The Vinayapitakam
and
Early Buddhist Monasticism
in its Growth and Development

Sukumar Dutt, M.A., B.L.

Originals

(an imprint of Low Price Publications)
Delhi-110052

Distributed by
D.K. Publishers Distributors (P) Ltd.
4834/24, Ansari Road, Darya Ganj,
New Delhi-110002
Phones: 51562573, 51562575, 51562577
e-mail: dkpd@del3.vsnl.net.in
visit us at: www.dkpd.com

Recomposed and Published
with a New Foreword 2007

ISBN 81-88629-44-8

Published by
Originals
(an imprint of Low Price Publications)
A-6, Nimri Commercial Centre,
Near Ashok Vihar Phase-IV,
Delhi-110052
Phones: 27302453
e-mail: lpp@nde.vsnl.net.in
visit us at: www.lppindia.com

Printed at
D K Fine Art Press P Ltd.
Delhi-110052

Introduction

It is not yet time to dilate on the importance of the subject of the present thesis in ancient Indian history. The history of ancient India is still in the making: it is yet "in a temporary vagueness of outline, as of things half-seen and processes half-realised." Yet the assertion may be confidently made that, as the whole economy of ancient India life and culture is more intimately realised by us, the important place of Buddhist monasticism in it will appear with increasing clearness. Its external relations its influences on society at large, it contributions to cultural history—all these topics are yet in the dream land of theory. Buddhist monasticism itself has been, like all other historic institutions, a gradual process, changing under pressure of its sociological environments and its own inner principle of evolution. Buddhist monastic life in India as pictured to us in the records of the Chinese travellers is far different from the monastic life that is reflected in the Vinayapitaka. The monasteries in the Chinese accounts have developed a new type: some of them are far-famed centres of learning. It is in this latter part of their history that we actually feel their importance and influence in ancient Indian life. We observe the monasteries gathering into themselves the rich and varied intellectual life of the period. The monasteries at Amarāvatī, Nālandā, Odantapura, Vikramasilā and Jagatdala appear like so many universities with their full complement of libraries, schools of studies, lecture-halls, professors and students flocking from all parts of Asia, far and near. No student of ancient Indian culture can fail to be struck with one feature which stands out in its later period, *viz.*, the continual interpenetration of Brahmanical and Buddhistic elements. There is reason to think that the great Buddhist universities were the channels for the commingling of different elements in the intellectual life of ancient India.

The growth of these universities however seems to have been arrested mainly by the violence of Mahomedan invasions. The storming of Behar and the wholesale massacre of monks at the place in or about 1197 A.D. by Kutubuddhin's general, Mahammad, which one of the survivors of the attacking party related so graphically to the historian Minhaz,[1] was probably a typical act of brute fanaticism. It seems at any rate that Buddhist monasticism, after the Mahomedan violence, disappeared below the surface of Indian life. But though 'passing through untold varieties of being,' it seems never to have lost the secret of its vitality in the place of its birth. Recent researches have brought to light the existence of living Buddhism in Bengal and Orissa even at the present day.[2] Whether Buddhist monachism, as distinct from the Buddhist religion, has similarly lived on among us in disguise is another question, though by no means an impossible one. For a Buddhist Order was founded in Orissa within living memory by one Bhima-Bhoi Araksitadāsa, and some little-known Oriyan manuscripts, seem to echo faintly and distantly the monastic laws of the Vinayapitaka.[3] It is one of a few indications to show that ancient Buddhist Monasticism, though submerged since the establishment of Mahomedan rule, did not die out at any time and the old monastic life never completely passed out of men's memory.

The splendid isolation of Ceylon has served to safeguard the old type of monastic life in that island. Being cut off from the multiple currents and cross-currents of thought and influence which largely transformed Buddhism in India itself, Ceylon has been able to preserve to a great extent its primitive character of the pre-Mahāyāna type. But Ceylonese monachism has an independent history of its own which is recorded in the Mahāvansa and the Dīpavansa. Although the ancient type remains fixed in Ceylon, its present monastic life cannot of course be regarded as a replica of North Indian monasticism of two thousand years ago—for account must be taken of the long process of time.[4] Even in changeless Asia, the nimble Time-spirit makes slow and imperceptible variations and Matthew Arnold's picture of the East in the oft-quoted stanza of *Obermann once More* is fading away before the 'gladsome light' of modern researches.

It seems to me that Spence Hardy, writing in 1850, did not fully realise this point. He has too often identified *Eastern Monachism* with the monachism of modern Ceylon. This indefatigable Wesleyan missionary who landed in the 'beautiful island,' as he affectionately calls it, of Ceylon in 1825, gathered a vast and miscellaneous knowledge of Buddhism from Singhalese manuscripts; he learnt from personal observation the habits and practices of modern Ceylonese monks; he observed many remarkable parallelisms between them and medieval monastic institutions of Europe, and when he brought out his work on *Eastern Monachism* in 1850, it was with all the justifiable enthusiasm of a new discovery. But Spence Hardy's information was derived from books current among Ceylonese monks which included promiscuously many ancient Pali books in Singhalese versions, as well as many Buddhist manuals in Elu, an ancient Ceylonese dialect, and of evident Ceylonese origin, and many works in Singhalese of the same origin of a comparatively modern date. These books were supplemented by stories and legends rehearsed to him by the monks. He treated all the works as being of the same value and never attempted to discriminate between the fundamental ancient rules of the Vinayapitaka and the later accretions that have been added to them in Ceylon. In each chapter of his work this shortcoming will be observed,—the Rules of Novitiate, for example, which he quotes from the manual of *Dina-Cariyāwa* are not of the Vinayapitaka and are of no historical antiquity. Spence Hardy's *Eastern Monachism* in fact does not reflect at all the monastic life that prevailed in Northern India two thousand years ago. But Hardy himself was not slow to recognise the second-hand character of the miscellaneous and, one may be pardoned for saying, ill-sorted information embodied in his work. "I am," says he with commendable humility, "like one who has met with individuals who have visited some Terra Incognita, and are able to describe it; they have placed before me their stores of information, and I have sifted them with all acumen I possess; and the result of my searches are embodied in these pages. But they who study the original canon may be regarded as actually entering the land, and winning here and there a portion of territory, more or less extensive; and by and bye the whole region will be gained, when the initiatory labours I am now pursuing will be forgotten, as they will have been succeeded by more authoritative investigations."[5] The basis of such authoritative investigations was laid by Oldenberg by the publication in 1879-83 of the five volumes of the Vinayapitaka, the codex of Buddhist monastic laws, and one who wanted to investigate the subject before the publication of Oldenberg's monumental work had to rely on unshifted and unclassified manuscripts, often misleading and unreliable. Yet Spence Hardy's 'preliminary survey' is a work of signal merit. He has clearly brought out the main features of Buddhist monastic life from study and personal observation, though it was not within the range of his resources to co-ordinate them, to exhibit their internal and external relations, and to throw them into the right perspective of history. It is only here and there and by rare flashes that Spence Hardy is able to introduce the all-important historical point of view.

After spence Hardy's 'initiatory labours' many popular works on Buddhism have come into the field. Our journey through Hardy's *Terra Incognita* has been made easy and familiar. In the company of pleasant and luminous writers like Rhys Davids, Oldenberg, Kern and others, one need not make the pilgrimage to the shrine of Buddhistic knowledge with peas in the boots and a hair-shirt on the back. But the extensive territory that has only been opened up needs to be explored inch by inch. The important historical materials in which Buddhist canonical literature is co-extraordinarily rich must be carefully sifted, and for this purpose 'comprehensive views' are often worse than useless. Unfortunately however a certain backwardness is kept up by the authors of hand-books and treatises by their habit of threading together, as it were all the three Jewels of the Buddhist Triad. But this comprehensive treatment of Buddhism by broad compartments, giving first a legendary biography of Buddha, then a rapid sketch of Buddhist doctrines, and lastly a static account of the Buddhist Order is by no means scientific history.

Sir Alfred Lyall has pointed out in one of his addresses[6] that "the tendency of the twentieth century is unfavourable to the artistic historian." The change from the artistic to the scientific school of historians, though Lyall regrets it, is accepted by him as a fact. The scientific writing of history, as he says, "based upon exhaustive research, accumulation and minute sifting of all available details, relentless verification of every statement," is destined to "gradually discourage and supersede the art of picturesque composition." "What," asks Lyall, "has been the effect of the altered situation upon the writer of history at the present time?" And his answer is—a narrowing of each historian's scope of operations. The modern historian must now "peg out his small holding and keep within its bounds." Those writers who aspire to traverse the whole vast area of Buddhism, even of the Pre-Mahāyāna, period of it, have become an anachronism to-day. Lord Acton in his published papers has a note of 'Advice to Persons about to write History,' of which the first word is *Don't*.[7] The advice of Lord Acton, echoing as it does the advice of *Punch* with regard to a quite different matter, is specially recommended to those who attempt at comprehensive treatment of Buddhism.

Another besetting vice of the current treatises on Buddhism is the straying away from the historian's strict point of view. The genuine historian must seek for the origins of historic institutions in the material environments of life and society, and the operation of ideas is significant to him in as much as it animates, accelerates or retards the material process of growth, development and decay of institutions. But Buddhism has too often been approached not from this historical standpoint, but rather from the philosopher's point of view, exaggerating the evolution of ideas and minimizing the material factors that made that evolution possible and determined its character. Hence it is that the ancient Buddhist Sangha through which Buddhism actually developed has received far less than its due share of attention. But it is in the growth and development of the Buddhist Sangha that the history of Buddhism remains embodied, and apart from the organisation of monastic life and community, ancient Buddhism is at best an abstraction, interesting more to the philosopher than to the scientific historian.

The tendency to comprehensive treatment and the bias for the philosopher's standpoint which prevail among writers on Buddhism have resulted in the static view of early (Pre-Mahāyāna) Buddhist Dhamma and Sangha. On reading, for instance, the meagre accounts of the Buddhist Sangha, out of all proportion to the importance of the subject, in the popular pages of Rhys Davids, Oldenberg, Kern and other writers, one is easily led to think that it was of a fixed type from the beginning; that most, if not all, of its laws came into existence at one birth, completely laid down by Buddha (?) as the canonical writers, committed to a theory which will be explained in Chapter I, would have us believe; and that its organisation was essentially of the same fixed character for five hundred years till the rise of the Mahāyāna. Nothing can be more erroneous than this static conception of early Buddhist community. The following pages of this thesis will show that neither was the Sangha in a perpetual state of arrested progress nor were its laws like 'the law of the Medes and Persians, which altereth not.' The early Buddhist communities on the other hand had a remarkable capacity for growth, development, variation, adjustment and progress. A necessary corrective to the current static view has been supplied in the following pages by adhering to the strict historic method. So the Pre-Mahāyāna Buddhist communities in their gradual evolution, which will be shown to be clearly traceable in ancient Pali literature, has been the subject of my enquiry in the present thesis.

Chronology has been truly called 'the eye of history'. In studying the ancient history of India, however, in any of its aspects, we have to proceed without its help by feeling our way cautiously through a mass of disordered materials. The clue that we must steadily follow is the succession of social conditions—that 'inner chronology' which the method of sociology adheres to. It is still possible for the historian to unravel from the tangled skein of our ancient literature the long threads of succession and evolution. Facts, legends and ideas which lie in them in a confused heap together may be thrown, with greater or less completeness, into evolutionary series which would point to a regular process of development. This method of study will necessarily admit certain elements of hypothesis and conjecture. But these elements cannot be excluded from the study of ancient Indian history in the absence of definite datable events. I have therefore attempted in the present thesis to trace only the process of development of the early Buddhist monastic communities instead of trying vainly to settle a time succession of events. The history of Buddhist monasticism, which is indeed a subject of vast proportions, may be broadly divided into two periods corresponding to the accepted division of the history of Buddhism, *viz.*, Hīnayāna (600 B.C.—100 B.C.?) and Mahāyāna (100 B.C.—1200 A.D.). The division of Hīnayāna and Mahāyāna, it must be understood, is always a tentative one and does not indicate any succession of stages of development. The original Hīnayāna form of Buddhism and the later Mahāyāna existed in India, for long centuries, side by side, reacting no doubt on one another, coming in contact at many points and also possibly amalgamating in parts. The inter-relation between the two is one of the vexed and unsolved problems of Buddhist history. But the distinction, so far as it goes, is clear enough for practical purposes and may be accepted for what it is worth. Now, recognising this distinction, we may set the limits of the period dealt with here as 600 B.C.—100 B.C., *i.e.*, the period of Buddhism before the rise of the Mahāyāna.

For this period our materials for the reconstruction of Buddhist monastic history, which are contained in the Vinayapitaka, are fairly complete. Further researches will no doubt throw light on this remarkable codex and its laws will become more and more clear to us as our knowledge of ancient Indian history increases. In Chapter I, I have sought to explain how the Vinayapitaka and its laws should be interpreted. Under the method of interpretation which I have suggested the

Vinayapitaka will clearly reflect to us a process of development in early Buddhist monasticism. The static view of it will be found to dissolve into a truer conception of the dynamic process of its growth and development.

Some of the topics that have come up in the course of the present dissertation have a wider bearing and deeper significance. Within the limits of my subject and treatment, it has not been possible for me to deal with them in an exhaustive manner as I should wish to. They are eminently worthy of further researches. I enumerate below some of these topics.

(i) The analogy between the Vinaya rules and the Greek Themistes as they are interpreted by Sir Henry Maine. (Chapter I)

(ii) The possible non-Aryan origin of the Paribrajaka institution. (Chapter II)

(iii) The constitution of non-Buddhist Sanghas and Ganas in ancient times. (Chapter VI)

(iv) The origins of the institutions of polity of the early Buddhist Sanghas. (Chapter VI)

(v) The positive state-enforced character of the laws contained in the Vinayapitaka. (Chapter VI)

The Chapter on *The Internal Polity of a Buddhist Sangha* may throw some side-light on the ideas of law and legal procedure in ancient India—a subject which has been approached up till now from the Brahmanical point of view of the Smritis.

List of Books Consulted

1. Oldenberg's Vinayapitakam—5 Vols.
2. The Vinaya Texts (S.B.E.).
3. B.S. Sastri's Pātimokkham (with Bengali translation).
4. The Digha Nikāya (P.T.S.)—3 Vols.
5. Rhys Davids's The Dialogues of the Buddha—2 Vols.
6. Steinthal's Udānam (P.T.S.).

7. Strong's Translation of the Udāna.
8. The Anguttara Nikāya (P.T.S).
9. Aung and Rhys Davids's The Points of Controversy (P.T.S.).
10. Tenckner's Milindapanho.
11. The Questions of Milinda (S.B.E.)—2 Vols.
12. Fausböll's Dhammapada.
13. Fausböll's The Sutta-nipāta.
14. Dhammapada and Sutta-nipāta (S.B.E., Vol. X).
15. Buddhist Suttas (S.B.E.).
16. Geiger and Tournour's Mahāwanso.
17. Senart's Mahāvastu—3 Vols.
18. Jaina Sutras (S.B.E)—2 Vols.
19. Hoernle's Uvāsagadasāo.
20. Satapatha-Brāhmana.
21. Āruneyopanishad; Jāvālopanishad; Brihadāranyakopanishad, etc.
22. Deussen's The Upanishads (The Religion and Philosophy of India).
23. Rig-Veda, X, 186; Atharva-Veda, XV.
24. Macdonell and Keith's Index to Vedic Names—2 Vols.
25. Iyengar's Life in the Age of the Mantras.
26. The Codes of Manu, Jājnavalkya, Vasista, Nārada, etc.
27. Kautilya's Arthasāstra (Mysore Government Publication).
28. Mukerjee's Vyavahāra-Mātrikā (Memoirs of A.S.B., Vol. III, No.5).
29. Dr. N.C. Sen Gupta's Sources of Law and Society in Ancient India (Calcutta University Publication).
30. Epigraphia Indica (Passim).
31. Jayaswal's Introduction to Ancient Hindu Polity (contributed to the Modern Review).
32. McCrindle's Ancient India at the Time of the Invasion of Alexander.
33. Vincent Smith's Asoka.

34. S.C. Vidyabhusan's So-Sor-thar-pa (J. and P.A.S.B., Vol. XI).
35. Hardy's Eastern Monachism.
36. Hardy's Manual of Buddhism.
37. Rhys Davids's Buddhist India.
38. Rhys Davids's Hibbert Lectures on Buddhism.
39. Rhys Davids's American Lectures on Buddhism.
40. Kern's Manual of Indian Buddhism.
41. Oldenberg's The Buddha.
42. Copleston's Buddhism, Primitive and Modern.
43. Scott's Buddhism and Christianity.
44. H.P. Sastri's Discovery of Living Buddhism in Bengal.
45. N.N. Vasu's Modern Buddhism in Orissa.
46. N.N. Vasu's Archæological Survey of Mayurbhanja, Vol. I.
47. Smith's Early History of India. (3rd Ed.).
48. Tylor's Primitive Culture (1893), 2 Vols.
49. Clodd's The Primitive Man.
50. The Cambridge Medieval History, Vol. I (Chapter on Monasticism).
51. Encyclopædia Britannica (11th Ed.)—On Confession.
52. The Oxford New English Dictionary—On Sect and Order.
53. Gasquet's The Rule of Saint Benedict (The King's Classics Series).
54. Colenso's The Holy Communion.
55. Maine's Ancient Law.
56. Oppert's The Original inhabitants of India.
57. Oman's The Mystics, Saints and Ascetics of India.
58. Max Müller's The Origin of Religion.
59. Max Müller's The History of Sanskrit Literature.
60. Introduction to Takakasu's I-Tsiang.
61. Lyall's Studies in History and Literature.
62. Acton's Historical Essays and Studies.

63. Salmond's Jurisprudence.
64. Several Articles and Translations in the following Journals:
    Indian Antiquary.
    Journal of Royal Asiatic Society.
    Journal of Asiatic Society of Bengal.
    Journal of the Buddhist Text Society (now defunct).
    Vienna Oriental Journal.
65. Anandagiri's Sankara-Vijaya (Jivananda Vidyasagar's Ed.).

References

1. See Raverty, p. 552—Tabakat-i-Nasiri.
2. See H.P. Sastri's Discovery of Living Buddhism in Bengal (1897) N.N. Vasu's Modern Buddhism and its Followers in Orissa (1911); Archæological Survey of Mayurbhanja (1911), pp. civ-cclxiii.
3. Bhima-Bhoi Araksitadāsa founded the Mahima Dharma in 1875. The *maths* of this sect are scattered in several villages of Mayurbhanja and round about. Vasu says in his Modern Buddhism (pp. 174-5): "Of the twelve or thirteen ascetic rules mentioned in the Buddhistic Scriptures the Mahimadharmin monk has even up till now been observing the rules of *Pindapātika, Sapadanacarika, Ekāsanika, Pattapindika* and *Khalu-pacchābhakīika*; but these are never found to be observed by Vaishnava monks or ascetics or those of any other sect."
4. Dr. Copleston says about Ceylonese monachism in his book on *Buddhism, Primitive and Modern*—"In short there is little or no idea of even aiming at the standard of monastic life which the Vinayapitaka exhibits. In certain points the rule is observed, for instance, in the ritual of admission, of full profession (*Upasampada*) and of confession. But the substance of the rule is ignored, not only in technical details, but in almost all that concerns the practical objects and the higher aims for which the community professes to exist." (p.267) Allowance must of course be made for the prejudice of the writer who was Lord Bishop of Calcutta.
5. See Preface to Hardy's *Eastern Monachism* (1860), p. viii.
6. Lyall's *Remarks on the Reading of History* (Inaugural address to the Students of King's College for Women, University of London, October 8, 1909)—See *Studies in Literature and History* by Sir Alfred Lyall.
7. See *Historical Essays and Studies* by Lord Acton, p. 505.

Foreword

Vinayapiṭaka – The Foundation of Buddhist Way of Life

The earliest available Buddhist sacred literature written in Pāli language is known as Tripiṭaka which consists of three books. All the three books contain the *Buddhavacanas*, the teachings of Lord Buddha about the proper view of reality and way of life. Since they embody the teachings they are called *piṭaka* and since they are organically interrelated they are collectively known as Tripiṭakas. They constitute the sacred texts of the *Sthaviravādins* or *Theravādins*. They are (1) *Vinayapiṭaka*, (2) *Suttapiṭaka* or *Sūtrapiṭaka*, and (3) *Dhammapiṭaka* or *Abhidhammapiṭaka*. All the three contain important historical material apart from religious, legal, ethical, philosophical, sociological and psychological ideas and practices.

A brief account of each of the three piṭakas will be helpful to have a holistic view of the entire corpus of this literature.

(1)The *Vinayapiṭaka* contains rules for the organization and disciplines of the *Saṃgha*, the order of the monks and nuns. It has three parts. The first part is called *Suttavibhaṅga* which comprises 227 rules for the conduct of monks and a somewhat larger numbers of rules for the nuns. It discusses penances for the transgressions of these rules and for the atonement of sins resulting from omissions and commissions. The second part is known as *Khandhakas* which contain rules for the administration of the *Sangha*, for construction of *caityas* and *vihāras* and for the daily routine of the inmates. The *Khandhakas* are further divided into two parts, namely, *Mahāvagga* or larger division, and *Cullavagga* or smaller division. The third part is named *parivāra* pertaining to the modes of teaching of *Vinaya*.

(2)The *Suttapiṭaka* consists of five *Nikāyas*. The first *Nikāya* is referred to as *Dīgha-nikāya* which is a collection of major discourses on important topics like the Four Noble Truths etc. The second *Nikāya* is known as *Majjhima-nikāya* which is a collection of middle length discourses. The third *Nikāya* is *Anguttara-nikāya* which is a collection of *suttas* or dialogues in a numerical order. The fourth one is *Samyutta-nikāya* which is a collection of *suttas* thematically. The fifth *Nikāya* is known as *Khuddaka-nikāya* which is a collection of miscellaneous works.

(3)The *Abhidhammapiṭaka* consists of seven works which are systematic expositions of various topics dealt with in the *Suttapiṭaka*. They are in the form of philosophical and psychological analysis of phenomenal existence and the ultimate nature of the real. It comprises seven books. They are as follows:

i. *Dhammasangani*
ii. *Vibhaṅga*
iii. *Kathāvatthu*
iv. *Puggala-paññatti*
v. *Dhātu-kathā*
vi. *Yamaka*, and
vii. *Patthāna*

II

We may now undertake a detailed study of the contents of the *Vinayapiṭaka*.

The first part is the *Suttavibhanga* which deals with *Patimokkha* or the obligatory rules of discipline. It is focussed on the *Patimokkha-sutta*. It consists of 227 rules which were to be followed strictly by all the monks and nuns. It also discusses various circumstances in which a person commits offences under these rules and what constitutes an exception. The exemptions are stated in very general terms. For instance, if a monk has an unbalanced mind, or is the first in the *Samgha* to commit the offence, or if the circumstances are such that the breach of the rule is inevitable, he need not be considered guilty of the breach of any of the rules. The rules and the permitted exceptions were meant to regulate their life and maintain order in the *Samgha*. These rules were recited on full-moon and new-moon days in separate assemblies of monks and nuns in which the leader of the ceremony at the end of each sentence asked the persons present there if anybody had been guilty of transgression mentioned therein. It was a duty of the person to declare his or her faults of omissions and commissions. This ceremony of confession of guilt was known as *Uposatha*.

In the *Suttavibhaṅga* each sutta is explained word by word with the help of a story describing where and when the Buddha himself enjoined that rule. Depending upon the gravity and severity of the transgression of the rules the concerned person was either expulsed from the order or was asked to atone. The section of the *Suttavibhanga* dealing with the former is known as *Pārājika* and the section dealing with the latter is called *Pācittiyas*.

The second part of the *Vinayapiṭaka* is called *Khandhakas*. It has two sections known as *Mahāvagga* and *Cullavagga*. The *Mahāvagga* has ten sections and the *Cullavagga* has twelve sections dealing with major and minor rules respectively. Like the *Suttavibhanga* here also rules and precepts are introduced with stories depicting the time, place and occassion when these were promulgated by the Buddha. The *Mahāvagga* can well be described as the history of the development of the Buddhist thought.

The third part is called *Parivāra*. It is like a supplement to the main body of the *Vinayapiṭaka* for the purpose of its proper study.

All the disciplinary rules framed for the conduct and guidance of the Buddhist monks and nuns are collected in the *Vinaya*. Though initially formulated by the Buddha himself they must have also got evolved in later times with the growth and spread of Buddhism retaining the basic spirit of Buddha's teachings. It seems that the *Pātimokkha-sutta* was the earliest composition as a part of the *Suttavibhaṅga*. However, it must be made clear that the different parts of the *Vinayapiṭaka* were not composed in a strict chronological order.

Monasticism has been one of the salient features of the Buddhist way of life. The structure and functioning of monastery, though rigid and closed, it was democratic. Here we find perhaps the world's earliest forms of democratic mode of living. There was a rule of law based on situational requirements. The distinction between absolute and relative moralities does not hold good in the Indian context where dichotomies are not entertained. Here we have situational morality based on human nature (internal situation) and outer environment (external situation).

With the growth, spread and development of Buddhism the monastic life also underwent changes. This was because Buddhism being ecumenical in character. It has the remarkable capacity to change and adjust. But the basic framework and spirit remained unchanged. A study of *Vinayapiṭaka* itself evinces this fact.

The core of *Vinayapiṭaka* is the body of rules or laws which were formulated for the smooth, efficient and orderly monastic life. The present work by Dr. Sukumar Dutta deals with these laws, and the modes of their interpretation. It also deals with the need and modes of movement of the monks and nuns to preach the Dhamma. A detailed analysis of the ritual of *Pātimokkha* is given. In short the book is rich in contents and is valuable for understanding the important text of the *Vinayapiṭ aka*.

S.R.Bhatt

Former Professor and Chair

Department of Philosophy, Delhi University

MP-23, Pitam Pura

Delhi-110088 (India).

20-7-2005

Contents

1
The Laws of the Vinayapitaka and their Interpretation

The only clue to the chronology of the Vinayapitaka is afforded by the account of the Council of Vesali in the 12th Khandaka of Cullavagga. If we accept the arguments of Oldenberg and Rhys Davids, the Council of Vesali must be dated about the middle of the 4th century B.C., and the compilation of a complete codex of Vinaya rules not much earlier than that date.[1] But though the Vinayapitaka, in the form in which it has been preserved to us, shows a more or less symmetrical plan and design, and points unmistakably to a final diaskeuasis a little earlier than the Council of Vesali, its contents are by no means the work of an age. They consist in fact, as I expect to show presently, of earlier and later materials welded together by a theory. When these are rightly interpreted and thrown into their proper sequence, they afford us in their evident process of growth and development the key to the evolution of Buddhist monachism itself.

It is well-known that the history of religious mendicancy in India may be traced to remote antiquity. The religious mendicants formed a wide-spread, populous and influential community in northern India even in the 6th century B.C. They lived outside social and communal organisations, but they constituted by themselves a well-defined community. They had internal relations among themselves,—communal customs, recognised manners and usages, and distinctive ideas and practices. There were also numerous sectarian parties among them called Saṅghas or Gaṇas, and one of them which afterwards became most influential in history was led by the world-famous Prince of the Sakya clan. Now this Saṅgha which recognised Buddha as their leader partook no doubt of the general characteristics of all Paribrajakas and followed generally their common customs and usages. Many features of Buddhist monachism therefore point back to earlier times than the foundation of the Buddhist Saṅgha itself. Such are the Vassa, the Uposatha, many eleemosynary and domiciliary rules, and numerous minor regulations of Buddhist monastic life which however it is next to impossible for us to pick out and assort with any degree of certainty. It is obvious that the only way of doing it would be to compare them with the usages, manners, rites and practices recorded of the Jaina, Hindu and other Paribrajakas in their respective ancient literatures. But the records of the non-Buddhist Paribrajaka sects are unfortunately far less exhaustive and satisfactory than those of the Buddhists. The Buddhist Saṅgha however gradually differentiated itself from the others and their communal character became more and more distinctive with the lapse of time.[2] The first step in this process of differentiation was the drawing up of a special body of rules, the Pātimokkha, which supplied an external bond of union for the Buddhist Saṅgha which had rested hitherto mainly on a community of distinct religious faith.[3] From this starting-point Buddhist monachism followed its own course. But at the earliest stages the individualistic and eremitical ideal of the primitive Paribrajakas predominated in it and like the other Paribrajakas, the Buddhist Bhikkhus led a wandering life, without any fixed local habitation; cohesion or cenobium.[4] But the observance of the Rain-retreat was a custom observed by Paribrajakas of all classes. This custom among the Buddhist Bhikkhus led afterwards to the staking out of Āvāsas. These āvāsas, being originally intended for sojournment during the Vassa period, became later on places of domicile for the Bhikkhus. Each Bhikkhu came to belong to a particular domicile, was member of the Saṅgha resident there and derived his personal rights and privileges therefrom. The word, Saṅgha, signified later on not the whole body of Buddhist 'Bhikkhus of the four quarters,' but only a particular cenobitical society resident at an āvāsa. This state of things, as I shall have occasion to explain later on,[5] was one of the causes of the growth of those Buddhist sects which bear place-names, pointing to their origin and growth at different seats of canonical culture. In the following pages I shall trace in detail these various stages of the development of Buddhist monachism before the growth of the Mahāyāna. Now at all these different stages rules were made for the guidance of the life and conduct of the Buddhist Bhikkhus—some of which had simply been inherited by the Saṅgha, others might have been borrowed from other sects, while the rest were peculiar to the Bhikkhus,—though it is a matter of the most delicate difficulty to separate and assign them to the different heads. The rules of the Vinayapiṭaka have thus followed the course of evolution of Buddhist monachism itself and as such may be truly said to have an 'inner chronology.'

We need not presume that the compilation of the laws of the Vinayapiṭaka was carried out at one time. From the beginning we hear of persons in the Buddhist Saṅgha, called Vinayadharas, who concerned themselves with the study and exposition of the rules of Vinaya. The existence of such professors was the surest guarantee for the conservation and consolidation of monastic laws from generation to generation among the Buddhist Bhikkhus. A final diaskeuasis was no doubt made shortly before the Council of Vesali, for the lawyer-like manner, in which the moot-points were sought to be decided there, presupposed the existence of a complete codex no longer susceptible of additions or alterations. The result of this gradual process of consolidation was that in the final redaction earlier materials were jumbled up with the later. Laws which had grown obsolete were retained in the process, those which had become partially unsuitable were amplified and extended in their application, new ones came into existence, either through long-standing custom becoming self-conscious or through adoption by common consent, being necessitated by new conditions of monastic life. Thus the laws of the Vinayapitaka partake of a most varied character, as the following illustrations will show.

A good illustration of the obsolescence of monastic laws is found in a short series of rules in the Pātimokkha called *Sanghādisesa Dhammā.* In this section certain offences are enumerated over which the Saṅgha has eccresiastical jurisdiction. It is said that the Saṅgha in these cases can inflict the prescribed penalty of Parivāsa and Mānatta *even against the will of the guilty Bhikkhu* (Jesam bhikkhu annataram vā annataram vā apajjitva yāvatiham janam paticchadeti tāvatiham tena bhikkhunā *akāmā* parivatthabbam, etc.). We know that in later times the disciplinary jurisdiction of the Sangha extended to not only over the Sanghādisesa, but also over all other offences, for the trial and punishment of which different forms of Sanghakammas were resorted to.[6] At this stage, it will appear that many of the Sanghādisesa Dhammā became obsolete. It will appear for example from Sanghā, 10, that the attempt to bring about a schism used to be considered an offence. If any Bhikkhu persisted in trying to create a schism inspite of repeated admonitions by the Sangha he made himself liable to the discipline of Parivāsa and Mānatta.[7] The same attitude towards schismatics is observed in Mahavagga, I, 67, where it is said that a schismatic must be expelled if he has been already ordained. As I shall point out later on, it was on this law that the Sarnath, Kosambi and Sanchi edicts of Asoka were based.[8] But the law relating to schismatics seems to have been very much relaxed later on. Accordingly we find that in Cullavagga, VII, 5.6, the intention to produce a schism is held to be not blame-worthy, but only such intention as was positively dishonest (*Ibid.*, 5).[9] Evidently a wider latitude for extreme differences of opinion was given in the later democratic Sanghas than in the earlier. In the 13th Sanghādisesa again we find the penalties of Parivāsa and Mānatta provided for those sinful Bhikkhus who corrupt lay men, but later on the *Pabbajaniya Kamma* is substituted for them.[10] This latter form of penalty is recognised even in the Vibhanga commentary on that rule. Again in a list of transgressions enumerated in Cullavagga, I, 1.1, for which the *Tajjaniya Kamma* should be carried out, we find certain offences which came specifically under the head of the Sanghādisesa Dhammā and for which, according to the older practice, Parivāsa and Mānatta should have been carried out. The offending Bhikkhus are described *inter alia* as *Vivādakāraka* (for which there is provision in Sanghā, 10 and 11) and *Sanghe Adhikaranakāraka* (for which there is provision in Sanghā, 8 and 9). Yet it is said in Cullavagga, I, 2.1, that the *Tajjaniya Kamma* is not intended for Parajika and Sanghādisesa offences. It is natural to think that many of the Sanghādisesa Dhammā lost their force and application at a later stage when the various Sanghakammas were devised. These illustrations from the Sanghādisesa Dhammā are sufficient to indicate that in the Vinayapitaka there are many laws which had become wholly or partially obsolete when the codex was finally put together. All the rules were not of the same operative force.

While on the one hand obsolete rules were thus retained, many of the old rules were recast and rehandled—either they were clearly defined or amplified as necessary or even refined away by a process well-known to lawyers as legal fiction. We have already referred to Sanghādisesa, 13. It is laid down in that rule that the Bhikkhus should ask one who, living near a village or a town, corrupts lay people and whose evil practices are overt, to depart from the āvāsa to which he belongs. Should he refuse to do so, on this adjuration being repeated thrice, he becomes guilty of Sanghādisesa and is consequently liable to Parivāsa and Mānatta. In Cullavagga, I. 13, *et seq.*, this rule is more precisely defined and amplified. The adjuration, mentioned in Sanghā. 13 is developed into a regular Sanghakamma and the penalties of Parivāsa and Mānatta are replaced by the penalty of banishment, pronounced in a solemn form. In Nissaggiya Pācittiya, 1, it is said that an extra robe might be kept by a Bhikkhu for a period of ten days after the settlement of the robes and the taking up of Kanthina. This period of limitation is more clearly defined later on in the light of the well-known legal distinction between custody and possession. The period of limitation, it is said in Mahavagga, V. 13, 13 (end), will begin to run not from the time when the Bhikkhu may have the robe in the custody of another, but when he has it in his personal possession. Numerous other instances may be cited where the old rules of the Pātimokkha are merely defined, amplified and illustrated in the Mahavagga and the Cullavagga, which shows clearly that the Vinayadharas in the Buddhist Sangha were no mean lawyers. Another mode was the suspension of the old Pātimokkha rules either as a temporary measure (as in Mahavagga, VI, 32. 1-2) or permanently during a prescribed period (as in Mahavagga, VII, 1. 3). By admitting numerous exceptions, many old rules were also amplified and their scope extended of which illustrations are too numerous to mention. Lastly that most remarkable agency by which old laws are everywhere brought into harmony with existing conditions of society, *viz*., Legal Fiction, also came into play in the development of monastic laws. In Ch. VII of the present thesis will be explained one of the most curious instances of legal fiction in the Vinayapitaka by which the old Pātimokkha rules of mendicancy were ameliorated to suit the conditions of the Buddhist cenobitical societies of later days. Other minor instances will also occur in the course of the present dissertation. So much about the development of the old Pātimokkha rules.

But side by side with this manipulation of old rules, we have the growth of new laws and regulations necessitated by the progressive development of the Buddhist Sangha. Some of these new rules, not found at all in the Pātimokkha, were no doubt the expression of old custom in the sense that the rule had been followed unconsciously and as a general practice till at a certain time, owing to some flagrant deviation from it or some other reason, it attracted notice and was formally enjoined. The minor rules about dress, manner of begging, etiquette, etc., seem to belong to me to this category and they occupy a considerable space in the Vinayapitaka. Many of these rules seem to have been intended only to preserve the outward distinctive signs of the Buddhist Bhikkhus and to prevent them from being mixed up with other Paribrājaka sects, such as the prohibition against making a begging-bowl out of a skull like the Pisācillikas,[11] or going naked like the Acelakas, or clad in garments of grass, of bark, etc., like (probably-) the Brahmanical and other Paribrājakas.[12] These rules and regulations would make up a formidable catalogue and they were evolved along with the development of a distinct character of the Buddhist Bhikkhus, who came to be separated later on altogether from the Paribrajakas.[13] But the more important of these new rules were those which were developed in the process of growth of the Buddhist cenobium relating to domicile, communal organisation, constitutional rights, congregational religious ceremonies, etc. Now, it must be clearly borne in mind that after the decease of the first Satthā, the Buddhist Sangha adopted no such principle of hagiology as for instance the Jainas.[14] There was therefore properly speaking no vested law-making authority anywhere in the Buddhist Sangha and any rule which might somehow obtain currency was likely to be adopted as a law of monastic life. The compilation of a complete codex of monastic laws was probably urged on by this among other considerations. The Pitaka was set up as a recognised standard of reference. But before this authoritative compilation, what were the sources of new laws? The dicta of Buddha as the only source of monastic laws was, as I shall presently show, an orthodox theory developed later.

A flood of light is thrown on the solution of the question raised above by a passage in the *Mahāparinibbāna Suttanta.* In IV, 7, are mentioned four Māhapadesas. They are spoken of as the probable sources of Dhamma and Vinaya, and it is said in the following sections that any doctrine or rule (Dhamma or Vinaya) emanating from any of these four Mahāpadesas should be carefully checked by comparison with the Sutta and the Vinaya.[15] These standards of reference can signify only the *Suttapitaka* and the *Vinayapitaka,* which superseded, in the middle of the 4th century B.C., all the material sources of monastic laws which are called in the *Mahāparinibbāna Suttanta* the Mahāpadesas. These are—

(*i*) Direct promulgation by Buddha, when the Bhikkhu proposing the rule is able to say—Sammukhā me tam āvuso Bhagavato sutam, etc.[16] That this source of law was a recognised one is attested by a curious instance. After the Council of Rajagaha where, according to tradition, the canon was settled, the Thera Bhikkhus approached Purāna and asked him to accept the Sangiti settled by them. Purāna refused them politely saying. Susangīt' āvuso therehi dhammo ca vinayo ca, api ca yath' eva mayā bhagavato sammukhā sutam sammukhā patiggahitam tath' evaham dhāressāmīti.[17] This saying of Purāna, by the way, is one of a few indications to show that the canon was not finally settled at the Council of Rajagaha. It will be observed that the words of Purāna are almost the same as are used in defining the first Mahāpadesa in the *Mahāparinibbāna Suttanta*

(*ii*) Promulgation of a rule by a Sangha containing elderly and leading men at an āvāsa. Thus for instance we hear of a rule being promulgated by the Sāvatthiya Sangha that Pabbajjā should not be conferred during the period of Vassa (Mahavagga, III, 13.1).

(*iii*) Promulgation of a rule by a number of elderly and learned Bhikkhus versed in canonical lore at an āvāsa. It was in this way, it will be observed, that five hundred Bhikkhus promulgated the complete body of Vinaya rules at the Council of Rajagaha. Their legislative authority had evidently no other basis than the third Mahāpadesa.

(*iv*) Promulgation of a rule by some learned professor of the canon at an āvāsa.

All these sources of monastic laws, called by the technical name of Mahāpadesas or Great Authorities, were superseded later on by the settled texts of the Pitakas which were necessitated by the fact that these material sources of law had become gradually obsolete. It is not difficult to understand how they became obsolete when we look into the matter a little closely. The first Mahāpadesa, for instance, could not be a living source of law after the decease of Buddha and his immediate disciples. The second one became more or less inoperative with the growth of the idea of the distinctness of each āvāsa which has been explained in the present thesis in Chapter V. Each Sangha was regarded later on as a separate and self-contained community and each āvāsa a distinct self-governing colony of Bhikkhus. The rules promulgated at one āvāsa for the Sangha resident there could therefore have no comprehensive operation. As regards the third, it will readily be seen that with the diffusion of Buddhist monasticism over larger and larger parts of the country, separated by long distances, with no modern facilities which annihilate time and space for us, the calling of such paramount synods as had been called once at Rajagaha became a matter of extreme practical difficulty. A Council of Rajagaha was possible only in a short time after the death of Buddha when Buddhist Bhikkhus were spread over a comparatively small area. The fourth could have only a precarious existence in conjunction with the idea of the equality of all Buddhist Bhikkhus at an āvāsa, which, as we shall have occasion to explain in Chapter VI, was one of the most dominant notes of early Buddhist monasticism. It was mainly by way of a Sanghakamma, following on a Vivādādhikarana, that a rule of law could be made binding on a Sangha, unless a Vinayadhara propounded a rule and the Sangha accepted it implicitly. These old sources of law were ultimately set at rest by the final compilation of the Vinayapitaka. If a question arose afterwards, *e.g.*, whether the 'horn-salt license'[18] was allowable?—It could not be urged, "From the mouth of Buddha, I have heard it," or "It has been promulgated by such and such a Sangha," or "It has been decided by such and such a company of Theras," or "It has been allowed by such and such a professor of law," but the chapter and verse of the Vinayapitaka must be quoted, as is done throughout at the Council of Vesali. When a new rule was proposed which had nothing corresponding to it in the Vinayapitaka, its legitimacy, as is said in Mahavagga, VI, 40.1, would depend on the question as to whether it was Kappiya (proper) or not. This might give rise to a Vivādādhikarana in the Sangha where the rule had been proposed and the resolution upon it could bind only the particular Sangha itself. In the light of this fact, the existence of various redactions of Vinaya rules, emanating from different schools, becomes easily explicable. They were settled at different āvāsas which had latterly become distinct and separate seats of canonical culture and the nurseries of Buddhist sects.

In his book on *Jurisprudence,* Salmond says, "The expression, source of law (*fons juris*) has several meanings which it is necessary to distinguish clearly. We must distinguish in the first place between the formal and the material sources of the law. A formal source is that from which a rule of law derives its force and validity. It is that from which the authority of the law proceeds. The material sources, on the other hand, are those from which is derived the matter, not the validity of the law. The material source supplies the substance of the rule to which the formal source gives the force and nature of law."[19] Bearing this distinction in mind, we may call the Mahāpadesas the material sources of Buddhist monastic laws, and that they were accepted and recognised as such is proved by the instances I have adduced above. The laws emanating from them would probably be accepted *ipso iure* as binding laws. But the authority and validity of these sources, as I have said, was gradually impaired by historical circumstances, though the laws coming from them had been conserved and consolidated by the Vinayadharas at many an āvāsa. A formal source of these extant laws, giving to them their force and validity, therefore became necessary and gained prominence. Just as the formal source of all civil law is its promulgation by the state, so the formal source of Buddhist monastic law was found in the theory of its promulgation by Buddha himself. It must be clearly realised that in the one case as in the other this formal source is only a theoretic notion. The rules of the Vinayapitaka were in point of fact derived from various material sources, but on each rule the theory was superimposed that it had been promulgated by Buddha on a certain occasion. To this theory all the canonical writers are piously committed: it is in fact the setting in which nearly all Buddhist rules and doctrines are cast in early Pali literature. The consequence of the systematic application of this theory has been that the evolved character of the laws of the Vinayapitaka has been transparently veiled by an orthodox theory of their origin. Rules which are inconsistent with each other and which clearly belong to different stages in the evolution of Buddhist monachism are thus placed on the same chronological level by putting them into the mouth of Buddha. This Buddha, the promulgator of monastic laws, is not any historical personage but only the embodiment of a theory, representing the formal source of all Buddhist laws and doctrines. An inadequate appreciation of this point is responsible for much of the confusion of thought which underlies many current histories of Buddhism.

Yet the theory, explained above, which dominates the entire corpus of Buddhist literature does not suffice to explain the form of a rule in the Vinayapitaka. Let us take an instance at haphazard to illustrate the form of a Vinaya rule. In Cullavagga, V, 33.3, a rule is laid down against the sneezing superstition. When a Bhikkhu has sneezed, the other Bhikkhus should not say to him 'Jīva' (Live). He who does so is guilty of a Dukkata. But it is permitted to say, 'Long Live,' to a house-holder on his sneezing. Now this rule is not simply laid down and attributed to Buddha. But the facts, real or supposed, and the reason on which the promulgation of this rule is based, are set out in detail. Many of such facts from which these rules follow are obviously inventions, as I shall indicate by a few illustrations later on. But what is important for us to consider in this connection is the stereotyped form of each rule—first, certain facts arise, then they are pressed on the attention of Buddha (this may be in any way—certain Bhikkhus do something and other Bhikkhus protest, or lay men protest, or certain facts come under Buddha's personal observation, or certain facts are reported to him, etc.), then follows the judgment of Buddha, embodying a rule, exactly covering the facts of the case. It will be observed that this form of laying down a rule of law has nothing analogous to it in Brahmanical legal literature: *it is in fact a form which precedes the era of codes.*

Sir Henry Maine, in his epoch-making work on *Ancient Law,* which has opened a new department of legal study, has said, "The conception of the Deity dictating an entire code or body of laws as in the case of the Hindu Laws of Manu, seems to belong to a range of ideas more recent and more advanced."[20] "The earliest notions," he says, "connected with the conception, now so fully developed, of a law of rule of life, are those contained in the Homeric words 'Themis' and 'Themistes.'"[21] Now the Greek Themis, as Maine explains it, was in effect nothing but "an authoritative statement of right and wrong in a judicial sentence after the facts, not one presupposing a law which has been violated." Themistes were thus "simply ADJUDICATIONS ON INSULATED STATES OF FACTS and did not necessarily follow each other in orderly sequence."[22] Maine regards the Greek Themistes, mentioned by Homer, as the most primitive form of enunciating any rule of life, and the fact is most remarkable that it is in this form that the rules of the Vinayapitaka are cast. Each rule purports to be a statement of right and wrong in a solemn judgment pronounced by Buddha after certain facts have arisen. He is therefore more a judge than a professed legislator. He pronounces on the validity of acts done by the Bhikkhus and does not profess to prescribe general courses of conduct for them.

We may take for example the following rules about foot-covering for the Bhikkhus in Mahavagga, V, of which there are fourteen:

(*i*) The use of shoes with one lining is enjoined. Shoes with double, treble or many linings are not to be worn on pain of *Dukkata* (1. 30 at the end).

(*ii*) Shoes that are all of blue, yellow, red, brown, black, orange or yellowish colour are not to be worn on pain of *Dukkata* (2.1).

(*iii*) Shoes that have edges of a blue, etc., colour are not to be worn on pain of *Dukkata* (2.2).

(*iv*) Many luxurious kinds of shoes which are enumerated are prohibited on pain of *Dukkata* (2.3).

(*v*) Shoes adorned with skins of different animals which are enumerated are prohibited on pain of *Dukkata* (2.4).

(*vi*) New shoes with linings are prohibited on pain of *Dukkata*, but cast off shoes with linings are allowed (3.2).

(*vii*) The wearing of shoes in the presence of unshod teachers and superiors is prohibited on pain of *Dukkata*. So is the wearing of shoes in the open ārāma (4.2).

(*viii*) The wearing of shoes in cases of disease in enjoined (5.2).

(*ix*) The use of foot-coverings is enjoined for one who wishes to get up on a couch or a chair (6.1).

(*x*) The use of foot-coverings is enjoined in the open ārāma and also of a torch, a lamp and a walking-stick (6.2).

(*xi*) The use of wooden shoes is prohibited on pain of *Dukkata* (6.4).

(*xii*) The use of shoes made of talipat leaves is prohibited on pain of *Dukkata* (7.2).

(*xiii*) Ditto of bamboo leaves (7.3).

(*xiv*) The use of shoes made of *Tina*-grass, etc. (all enumerated) is prohibited on pain of *Dukkata* (8.3).

Each one of these fourteen rules is said to have arisen *ex post facto.* To rule (*vi*), for instance, the following typical story is appended:—

Buddha, once on a time, went into Rajagaha accompanied by a Bhikkhu who walked limping. On seeing his condition a lay man took off his own shoes which had many linings and, approaching him, asked: (Mahavagga, 3. 1-2):

'Why does your reverence limp?'

'My feet, friend are blistered.'

'But here, Sir, are shoes.'

'Enough, good friend! shoes with many linings have been forbidden by the Blessed One.' (*Vide* No. 1).

On hearing this conversation, Buddha called upon the Bhikkhu to accept the shoes and having delivered a religious discourse, laid down the above rule (No. (*vi*)] for the Bhikkhus. The rule is properly an adjudication, a pronouncement on certain facts, prescribing a single act, *viz.*, the wearing of shoes of a certain kind when they are cast-off. Now all the fourteen rules, containing injunctions, prohibitions and permissions, might have been gathered up, as in a modern rule of law, into one comprehensive formula laying down the kinds of shoes allowable and the occasions for their use and thus prescribing a general course of conduct. But this is not done. Instead we have many distinct rules each embodying an adjudications on the facts as they arise on a particular occasion. The form is curious: the old Greek form of Themistes, which, according to Sir Henry Maine, is the most primitive form of laying down any rule of life.

If the analogy that I have pointed out between a Greek Themis and a Vinaya rule be true, it may help us a good deal in understanding the Vinayapitaka. It becomes abundantly clear why the codex of Buddhist canon law is not in the form of a code. It enshrines in fact a fossilised relic of the mode of law-making prevalent in primitive societies. We understand also why a story was thought to be necessary to append to every law. In primitive conception every law being an adjudication and command, the 'state of facts' on which the adjudication was made could not be dispensed with in laying down the law. From this point of view, the Vinayapitaka is of immense value in the history of law, preserving, as it does, the most primitive jural notion, found only as a trace in Homer, which has worn out completely in later legal literature of Greece, Rome and India.

Now these 'states of facts' out of which the rules arise show a bewilderingly varied character. Some of the stories may have a kernel of historical truth which was borne down to later times on the current of persistent tradition. For some of the rules are so curious and unthinkable in character and arise so naturally out of the stories that one is tempted to attribute some truth to the fundamental stories. Others were only legendary stories to which the rules were artificially fitted in later times. Thus the whole legendary life-story of Jivaka is given at the beginning of Mahavagga, VIII, and rule only indirectly and incidentally connected with the story, is laid down at the end in Mahavagga, VIII, 2, 36. Of the other rules again it is extremely difficult to say whether the stories appended to them have any historical or legendary value. Thus for instance in Mahavagga, VI, 17.7, certain rules of mendicancy are relaxed and the story says that this was necessitated by scarcity of food prevailing at Rajagaha. These relaxations are expressly removed in 32.2, and the old rules of mendicancy are re-inforced, on the ground that no scarcity was then prevailing at Vesali, where the rules were re-inforced, 'the city being well-stocked with food, the harvest good, alms easy to obtain, and a living procurable, even by gleanings in the fields.' The two sets of rules, one abrogating the other, read together, might suggest that the Bhikkhus actually used to relax little the rigour of the rules of mendicancy by storing up food during times of scarcity, but afterwards this was felt to be not proper and the practice was generally given up. But this is purely conjectural and the stories might point to certain actual incidents. We next come to the stories which are obvious inventions made in order to base the rules upon them. Sometimes on the basis of the same story two different rules are grounded as in Mahavagga, VI, 9 and VIII, 17, and also in Cullavagga, V, 20. 1-2 and IV, 4. 8-9. Again the rule sometimes does not arise out of the story, at all or is very remotely connected with it, and numerous instances of this may be cited. Sometimes the inventive genius of the author seems to fail him and on the basis of very slender, featureless and commonplace stories whole manuals of conduct are given as in Mahavagga, VIII, I and V. Lastly we light upon stories which are the barest and the most commonplace possible, the narrative tending to the irreducible minimum, as in Cullavagga, V, 6, where the rule does not arise out of the story at all (which is simply this, that a Bhikkhu was bitten by a snake), and is given only to introduce a recipe for snake-bite. As matter of fact there is a great variety in the degree of adjustment between the rule and the story in the Vinayapitaka. But the stories, however slight and commonplace, were thought to be necessary, for the primitive jural notion was that a rule of conduct must needs be an adjudication on a certain state of facts.

But the stories, apart from the rules and by themselves possess a value of their own to the historical student. Apart from worthless invention, even those stories which are obviously legendary are valuable as letting us into the social, moral and mental atmosphere of the times in which they originated. Victor Hugo has well said, "History has its truth; legend has its truth. Legendary truth is of a different kind from historic truth. Legendary truth is invention with reality for result." These legendary stories of the Vinayapitaka therefore may well be received in illustration, though not in proof. But the character of each story must be cautiously sifted before it may be evaluated by the historian. Some of them have such a strong appearance of reality that they easily delude us into mistaking them for genuine history. An illustration may be taken from the story appended to the rule against the sneezing superstition which we have already referred to.

It is said that on a certain occasion when Buddha was delivering a sermon, he happened to sneeze, whereon there was such a mighty shout of. "Jīvatu bhante bhagavā Jīvatu sugato," that the discourse was interrupted. Buddha then explained to the simple-minded audience the futility of this benediction and laid down the rule against saying 'Jīva' after a sneeze by a Bhikkhu. But the rule was relaxed in favour of a householder the saying of 'Jīva' to whom by a Bhikkhu after a sneeze was allowed. The superstition condemned here is, as Tylor has pointed out,[23] one of the most persistent 'survivals in culture.' It exists in all countries in all ages. The lucky sneeze of Telemachos in the *Odyssey* called forth a shout of adoration to the gods along the ranks of warriors. Tiberius Cæsar, 'the saddest of men,'—so Pliny the historian tells us,—exacted a salute after a sneeze. The story of the sneezing of the king of Monomotapa and the shouts of blessings, passing from mouth to mouth in the city, is quaintly told by that philosophic observer of human errors, Sir Thomas Browne, in *Pseudodoxia Epidemica*. Whether among the civilized Greeks and Romans or the savage tribes of the Zulus, the Polynesians, the New Zealanders and the Samoans, whether in the east among the Indians or in the west among the Europeans, the sneezing superstition, descended from the primitive conception of 'soul' as *Anima* or Breath, flourishes in an equal degree. Now considering the world-wide and extraordinary prevalence of this superstition and its condemnation in the Vinayapitaka, one is naturally led to think that it was the work of a bold rational thinker who deprecated a popular and wide-spread superstition. We seem almost to come in touch with a personality behind the rule—a strong rational personality. But when we consider the rule in the light of the ideas prevalent among the Indian Sannyasis and Paribrajakas in ancient times, we observe that it is only one form of prevalent idea among them. The Buddhist rule allows that 'Jīva' may be said to a householder after a sneeze, and it is clearly implied that there is a certain difference in the ideas of the Sannyasis and Paribrajakas on which the exception is grounded.[24] We know that one of the fundamental ideas among the Paribrajakas was they should regard their bodies as carcases.[25] Even among the Sannyasis of the present time the idea in many forms and implications prevails. I have seen many Sannyasis who do not accept a salute on the ground "that a corpse may not be saluted."[26] I am reliably informed that the Sannyasis of any denomination do not say 'Jīva' after a sneeze. The idea may derive some of its strength also from the ancient Doctrine of Sorrow which is reflected in post-vedic Brahmanical Buddhist and Jaina literatures and which dominates the Indian mind even today. An attachment to and longing for life such as is implied in the benediction of Jīva is inconsistent with the principles of Sannyasi life. The Buddhist rules about the sneezing superstition may well be one of the many protean forms of a prevalent idea among the Paribrajakas and Sannyasis, the story and the reason being of later invention in support of a well-recognised practice. Thus the supposed personal authorship of the rule vanishes and our search after its origin ends not in a rational personality, but in a certain group of ideas.

The illustration given above serves as a much-needed caution against the hasty interpretation of any rule in the Vinayapitaka. In interpreting any Vinaya rule, the following points must be carefully considered and allowance made therefor:

(*i*) The orthodox theory which covers the diverse origins of the rules.

(*ii*) The common, primitive form in which all the rules are cast.

(*iii*) The place of any rule in question in the order of evolution of monasticism among the Bhikkhus.

(*iv*) The value of the story in relation to the rule which is ostensibly based upon it.

Unless we are prepared to take into consideration all these points we cannot presume to understand in their true light and bearing the laws of Vinayapitaka. Through an inadequate appreciation of the complexities of the problem, even many learned writers on Buddhism have been betrayed into fathering on the historic Buddha rules and regulations of his Order for which he could not possibly have been responsible.

References

1. "If, as justified by Asoka's inscriptions, we assume the year 265 B.C. as the approximate date of his coronation, and we calculate 118 years back from this to the Council as Vesali in accordance with the chronological system of the Ṃahavaṁsa and Dipavaṁsa—we shall find the date of this council of fall somewhere about 383 B.C. From what has been said above, the revision of the Vinaya must have been somewhere before that time, but not much earlier."—Oldenberg's *Vinayapitakam,* Intro., pp. XXXVIII-XXXIX. "It is sufficient for our present purpose to be able to fix the Council of Vesali, even after making allowance for all possibilities, at within thirty years of 350 B.C."—*Vinaya Texts,* S.B.E., Pt. I, Intro., p. xxiii.
2. See Ch. V of the present thesis, footnote 82.
3. See Ch. III of the present thesis.
4. *Ibid.*
5. See Ch. V of the present thesis.
6. See Ch. VI of the present thesis.
7. Jo pana bhikkhu samaggassa sanghassa bhedāya parakkameyya bhedanasamvattanikam vā adhikaranam samādāya paggyya titteyya * * * Sanghādisesa.
8. See Ch. VII of the present thesis, footnote 50.
9. See Ch. VII of the present thesis at the end.
10. See Cullavagga, I, 13 *et seq*. The translators say, "The whole of this chapter (setting out the offences for which the Pabbajaniya Kamma should be inflicted) recurs in the Sutta Vibhanga on the 13th Sanghādisesa. The proceeding here laid down is really a later method of acting under the circumstances similar to those for which that rule had previously been the authorised dealing."—*Vinaya Texts,* S.B.E., Part II, p. 347, footnote 1.
11. Cullavagga, V, 10.2 [The *Pisācā* are mentioned as a Sect (*Gana*) in *Milinda,* Tenckner, p. 191].
12. Mahavagga, VIII, 28, 1-3.
13. See Ch. V of the present thesis, footnote 82.
14. See Ch. VI of the present thesis (at the beginning).
15. *Cf.* Sutte otāretabbāni vinaye sandassetabbāni.

16. See *Mahāparinibbāna Suttanta,* IV, 8 (*Dighā-Nikāya*, P.T.S., Vol. II, p. 124).
17. See *Cullavagga,* XI, 1, 11.
18. Singilonakappo—which was raised at the Council of Vesali. See *Cullavagga,* XII, 2.8.
19. Salmond's *Jurisprudence* (Fourth Edition), p. 117.
20. Maine's *Ancient Law* (Edited by Pollock, 1909), p. 5. But Maine's characterisation of the Laws of Manu is not quite accurate, as every student of Hindu Law is aware.
21. *Ibid.*, p. 3.
22. *Ibid.*, p. 8.
23. See Tylor's *Primitive Culture* (1891), Vol. I, pp. 97-104.
24. Cf. Gihī bhikkhave mangalikā (Cullavagga, V, 33.3). But this reason suggests nothing. It is only an after-thought of supply a reason for an already existing practice.
25. See Deussen's *Upanishads,* p. 382.
26. This was what certain Sannyasis actually told me when I was going to salute them. They gave no authority for this reason on which they refused a salute.

2

The Primitive Paribrajakas—A Theory of their Origin

It is generally admitted that much of the earliest canonical literature of the Buddhists and the Jainas, whatever their actual chronology, reflect to us in faithful traditions the life and society of northern India in 6th century, B.C. It is not necessary for us to enter here into the elaborate arguments on which this view is based. But students of ancient literature know with what persistency traditions survive long centuries after the historical facts in which they originated have passed into oblivion. It is even possible in some cases to discover the original historical facts hidden in them by the search-light of historical criticism. This 'harking back' in ancient literature, once clearly perceived and intimately realised by the historian, helps to guide his steps beyond the chronological limits where written records come to a stop. Thus the Udāna seems to be a comparatively late Pali work in the Sutta pitaka. Yet the description of the Paribrajakas in the Jaccandhavagga (4,5,6) of the Udāna clearly points back to the teeming life of the Paribrajaka community in the lifetime of Buddha. They are described thus: "sambahulā nānātitthiyā samanabrāhmanā paribbājakā * * nānādiṭṭhikā nānākhantikā nānārucikā nānādiṭṭhinissayanissitā."[1] They enter Sāvatthi in a miscellaneous crowd for alms, putting forth many speculative doctrines of the same character, though not exactly the same, as those discussed in the Brahmajāla-suttanta, wounding one another with 'mouth-weapons' (mukhasatthihi). The whole passage is purely reminiscent and bears the stamp of an earlier age than the time when the Udāna itself was compiled, for there is reason to think that the Paribrajaka community did not contain so many sectarian varieties later on.

If then we take the Buddhist Pitakas and the Jaina Angas as representing North Indian life of the 6th century B.C. one notable feature of it stands out in relief. It is the existence of populous community of men who live outside the organisation of society. They are called by various names,—Paribbajaka, Bhikkhu, Samana, Yati, Sannyasi, etc.,—the last name however being seldom used in Buddhist and Jaina literature. They have one essential characteristic in common, *viz.*, that they are all professed religieux, homeless and nomadic. The standing phrase in the Pali scriptures for one who embraces this mode of life is—Agārasmā anagāriyam pabbajati. Hence in the following pages we have called all sorts of this wandering religious community by the general name of Paribrajaka. The character of this community is so varied and miscellaneous that it is extremely difficult to generalise upon it. They live by begging, have no settled dwelling (except during the rains when the observance of the Rainretreat is a common custom among them),[2] move about from place to place, and are either ascetics, practising austerities,[3] or are, to quote the words of Rudyard Kipling, 'dreamers and babblers of strange gospels.' No other common characteristics can be attributed to the community as a whole.

In this community of wandering religious men, a superior place is assigned to one class, called the Samanas. Thus in the Kāssapa-sīhanāda-sutta, the burden of the paragraphs, 15-17, setting out the higher ideal of religious life, is "From that time, O Kāssapa, is it that the Bhikkhu is called a Samana, is called a Brahmana." The superiority of the Samana is implied in Mahāparinibbāna Suttanta, 62, when Buddha says, in reply to Ananda, that there is no Samana in a dhamma wherein the 'Noble Eightfold Path' is not found. It is only the Samana moreover that is mentioned in the Pali works, in Jaina literature, in the Inscriptions of Asoka, etc., in juxtaposition with the Brahmana—a class of the Aryan society held always in the highest honour since the dawn of Indian history. The Samanas are represented as enjoying the same intellectual pre-eminence as the Brahmanas. The intellectual activities of both the Samanas and the Brahmanas are described, criticised and commented on in Buddhist and Jaina literature. In the Brahmajāla Suttanta, a number of philosophic speculations agitated among the Brahmanas and the Samanas are discussed and refuted. (The Jaina counterpart of this a Buddhist suttanta is found in the short section, entitled Freedom from Errors, in the Sutrakritanga in which a number of heretical theses are catalogued.)[4] In the Jaina Angas also samples of the speculative ideas of the Brahmanas and Samanas are given *passim*. In the Kāssapa-sīhanāda Sutta, the Samanas and Brahmanas are classified together as—Sila-vādā, Tapo-jigucchāvādā, Pannā-vādā, Vimutti-vādā,[5] and an account of their various ascetic practices is given. Instances may be easily multiplied from Buddhist and Jaina literature to show that the Samanas equally with the Brahmanas enjoyed intellectual pre-eminence with the people, being regarded as the chosen exponents of philosophic ideas and speculations current in that age.

The distinguished place that the Samanas held in the Paribrajaka community is recognised by outsiders also. People keep up gifts of piety to Samanas and Brahmanas alike.[6] The feeding of the Samanas and Brahmanas is recognised as a meritorious act;[7] they are feasted and entertained on auspicious days.[8] They are together mentioned as being worthy of respect and gifts in the Inscriptions of Asoka.[9] They are piously invoked along with other tutelary spirits for protection.[10] Both the Brahmanas and the Samanas go to the assembly convoked by the king and, being professors of religion, gain proselytes, who pay high honour to them, by explaining and teaching their religions.[11] Even a slave, it is said, when he becomes a 'pabbajita samano' is worthy of reverence by the King himself,[12] and Avantiputta, King of Madhurā, says to Mahākaccayana that he would extend to the Sudra the same honourable treatment as to a Kshatriya if both are Samanas, for the simple reason that in the life of the Samana caste distinctions do not subsist—yā hi'ssa bho kaccāna pubbe suddo ti samannā sā'ssa antarahitā, samano t'eva sankham gacchatīti.[13] The Buddhist scriptures represent kings as respectfully consulting not only Buddha but also other leading Samanas,[14]—though among them there were recruits from the untouchable classes and though we frequently hear of Sudras and Candālas becoming samanas.[15]

From all this evidence, it is quite apparent that the Sramanas enjoyed the highest status among the wandering community of religious mendicants. Among the Sramanas, there were leaders of sects and parties (*e.g.*, Nigrodha,[16] Sanjaya,[17] Uruvela[18] and others) and six of them are constantly referred to in Pali literature as 'sanghī ganī ganacāriyo.'[19] Many of these sects and parties are enumerated in Buddhist and Jaina literature, but these enumerations are difficult to understand and more difficult to reconcile with one another. One list occurs in a passage in the Anguttara to which Rhys Davids has drawn prominent attention.[20] It mentions ten sects—Ajivaka, Nigantha, Mundasavaka, Jatilaka, Paribbajaka, Magandika, Tedandika, Aviruddhaka, Gotamaka, and Devadhammika. We fall into hopeless difficulties in defining these sects, as they cross and overlap one another. A different enumeration is found later on in the Milindapanho[21]—Malla, Atona, Pabbata, Dhammagiriya, Brahmagiriya, Nataka, Naccaka, Langhaka, Pisāca, Manivadda, Punnavadda, Candima-suriya, Siridevata, Kalidevata, Siva, Vasudeva, Ghanika, Asipasa, Bhaddiputta. They are said to be so many Ganas (sects) and of them the Pisācā (under the name of Pisācillikā) are referred to in Cullavagga, V, 10, 2 and they certainly were a sect of religious mendicants as they are said to have carried begging-bowls made of skulls. As regards the other sects in the Milindapanho enumeration, we know nothing except what their names seem to import to us. The Jaina commentator Sīlānka (9th century, A.D.) quotes a very old hemistich in one of his glosses in which Samanas are classified as five—Nirgrantha, Sākya, Tāpasa, Gairika and Ājīvaka.[22] In the corpus of early epigraphical records of Northern India, we find mention only of the Buddhists, the Jainas and the Ājīvakas. (No mention is found of the last after the 2nd century, B.C.)[23] Now these enumerations of the mendicant sects that we may discover belong to different times and cannot be reconciled with one another. The confusion which underlies them is due to various causes—to partial and defective knowledge, inadequate appreciation of the distinction between genus and species, and confusion between tradition and personal knowledge. It is also extremely difficult to say how many of the sects enumerated by later writers go back to the 6th century, B.C.

Among these sects and parties there seems to have existed in primitive times a good deal of mutual intercourse. In the course of their constant peregrinations they frequently met together at rest-houses and also at common meeting-places specially built for them, one of which is even called a Debating Hall-samayappavādakasālā).[24] The effects of such mutual intercourse must have been considerable and are perceptible at any rate in the early history of Jainism in the borrowing of the rules of one sect by another and in the growth of new sects by fission. Jacobi[25] and Hoernle[26] have traced in Jainism borrowings from the Acelakas and the Ājīvakas and similar borrowings may no doubt be discovered in Buddhism also. Instances occur of the members of one sect going over to another or a secessionist party founding a new sect, as the Jatilakas become Buddhists, the followers of Sanjaya accept Buddha as their Satthā, Mahāvīra breaks with Mokkhali Gosāla,[27] as Devadatta with Buddha, founding a new sect. The primitive Paribrajaka sects were of a proselytising character and must have considerably influenced and modified one another with such facilities of mutual intercourse. Each of these sects had a clearly defined Dhamma of its own, but whether it had an equally clearly defined Vinaya, a special body of external rules, is another question which I have dealt with in Chapter III of the present thesis. Among all sects, as has already been said, it was the Sramanas who were entitled to the highest reverence.[28] The above is the general picture revealed to us of the Paribrajaka community of the 6th century, B.C. in the earliest Buddhist and Jaina canonical literature. This remarkable mendicant community have lasted down to our day and remained a constant factor in Indian history through all its chances and changes. They have excited the liveliest interest of all foreigners who came out to India at different times from 'Philip's warlike son' to Professor Campbell Oman in our day.[29]

The origin of this community of itinerant religious mendicants, of such hoary antiquity in India, is wrapped in obscurity. But European writers on Buddhism have sometimes put forward theories of their own which it will be necessary for us to examine carefully before propounding any other theory. We may take as typical the theories suggested by Rhys Davids, Max Müller, Deussen and Oldenberg.

1. Rhys Davids in his *Buddhist India* says with characteristic bias— "The intellectual movement before the rise of Buddhism was in a large measure a lay movement, not a priestly one."[30] The result of this 'lay movement,' he seems to think, was the growth of these wandering bodies of religieux, the Paribbajakas of Pali literature. This is a wide, vague, *à priori* theory, resting really on very slender foundation. In the first place, to speak of a general intellectual movement in Northern India immediately before the rise of Buddhism is one of the many misleading common places of ancient Indian history. There is nothing except the accounts of the intellectual activities of the Samanas in Buddhist and Jaina literature to prove that there was any intellectual movement, properly so called, in the immediate pre-Buddhistic age. Thoughts, ideas, philosophic speculations had no doubt broadened down from century to century among the intellectual section of the people, but whether there was any general 'accelertion' of intellectual life, giving birth to these wandering bodies of sophists and teachers among whom religious and philosophical questions were so earnestly and restlessly agitated, is an open question. To infer an intellectual movement from the abundance of religious wanderers and philosophic speculators in the 6th century, B.C., and then to account for their growth by the intellectual movement involves a '*petitio principii*.' In the second place, to point to an intellectual movement in any age necessarily implies a comparison with the preceding ages and such comparisons are impossible in ancient Indian history where we have no continuous records to build upon. If the same amount of materials which we have for the reconstructions of social life in the immediate pre-Buddhistic age were available for the age preceding it, we might possibly have come to a different

conclusion. There is therefore no sufficient warrant for propounding such facile theories as that of a pre-Buddhistic intellectual movement, and to do so would be, to adopt Rhys Davids' own metaphor, like playing chess '*sans voir,*' without seeing the pieces. The theory which is born of the notion that in the 6th and 5th centuries B.C., there was world-wide intellectual movement,[31] is thus a fruitless one for our purpose.

2. Paul Deussen sets great store by the practical results of the Upanisad theories of Tapas and Nyāsa.[32] But Deussen's argument may be applicable to only one section of the primitive Paribrajaka community, but not to the whole body, for many Paribrajaka sects, whose doctrines are known to us, did not recognise at all the very fundamentals of such theories, and were admitted on all hands to be openly anti-Brahmanical. In the Kāssapa-Sīhanāda-Sutta, a class of Sramanas and Brahmanas are called *Vimutti-vādā*. In this class probably are to be included the Brahmanical Yogis and Sannyasis whose religious activities were explicitly grounded on the theory of Vimutti (Vimukti) or Emancipation from which as Paul Deussen has shown, the practical results of Yoga and Nyāsa logically follow.[33] But the Vimutti-vādā among the Samanas constituted one class only and the Upanishad theories cannot account for the other classes of Paribrajakas who did not consider the Upanishad idea of Emancipation to be the *raison d'etre* of religious mendicancy. In Buddhist canonical literature for example the object and purpose of religious mendicancy is said to be nothing more than *Brahmacariya* (religiosity),[34] and the ideas of Tapas and Nyāsa are not at all suggested. The attachment to household life must be discarded, not because there is any special virtue in the mere rejection of it, but because worldly attachments are hindrances to religious living.[35] The Buddhist and Jaina religious mendicants never described themselves as Sannyāsin—the name which more frequently than any other describes this mode of life in the Upanishads. It cannot in fact be said that any one philosophic idea presided over the growth of the Paribrajaka institution,—for the speculative ideas which the Paribrajakas themselves profess are as widely various as the gnostic heresies of early Christian

Church which Charles Kingsley described as "a strange brood of theoretic monasters, begotten by effete Greek philosophy on Egyptian symbolism, Chaldean astrology, Parsee dualism, and Brahmanic spiritualism."[36] Religious mendicancy in India cannot in fact be traced to the materialisation of any one philosophic idea.

3. If there is any force in the arguments we have put forward above, the theory of the Brahmanical ascetic being the original of the Buddhist and Jaina religious mendicant would be no longer tenable. Max Müller in his *Hibbert Lectures,* p. 351, Bühler in his translation of the *Baudhayana Sutra,* S.B.E. (*passim*), Kern in his *Manual of Indian Buddhism* and Jacobi in his Introduction to the *Jaina Sutras,* S.B.E. (Pt. I, pp. xxiv-xxxii)—all contend that the Brahmanical ascetic was the model of the Buddhist and the Jaina. This may be true only in the sense that some of the rules of the Buddhist and Jaina Paribrajakas were probably borrowed from the Brahmanical Paribrajakas, which again is only a presumption raised by the fact, we have already referred to, of the mutual intercourse that existed among the Paribrajakas of different sects. But which of these rules were borrowed we can never ascertain. There existed a Paribrajaka community from remote antiquity in India and customs and practices among them were the common property of all sects. It is probable that the Buddhist Sangha among them was founded later than the sect of Brahmanical Paribrajakas. But the Brahmanical Sannyasis, the Buddhist Bhikkhus and the Jaina Srāvakas all belonged to the same ancient society of wandering religious mendicants, and it is obvious that among all the sects there should subsist a certain community of ideas and practices. The question of the origin of the institution of wandering religious mendicancy remains unsolved.

4. Oldenberg seems to find the solution in the popularising of philosophic speculations in the process of spreading from the Western schools among the simple and earnest people of the Eastern tracts.[37] This is also a wide and vague theory which however will appear to contain a certain element of truth.

It seems to me that the question has never been squarely faced in the proper historical spirit by any western scholar and hence the obscurity of *a priori* theories hangs heavily over it. An unbiassed enquiry however may tend somewhat to dissipate this obscurity and such an enquiry we propose in the following pages of this chapter. The manifestations of the 'other-worldly spirit' have been bewildering in their variety in ancient India and the idea which underlies this particular institution should first of all be dissociated from the other forms, like *Tapas* for instance, of this 'other-worldly spirit,'—and this basic idea is found in the stereotyped words, which describe one embracing the life of the religious mendicant and wanderer in Pali literature—*Agārasmā anagāriyam pabbajati*: it is homelessness for the sake of a higher spiritual life. This is the common attribute of all the Paribrajakas, whatever their sects, denominations, ideals and practices may be.

In the Rig-Veda, X, 136, certain Munis are described in the following verses:

केश्यग्निं केशी विष केशी बिभर्त्ति रोदसी ।
केशी विश्वं स्वर्द्दशि केशीदं ज्योतिरुच्यते ॥ (1)

Sāyana—केशाः केशस्थानीया रश्मयः तद्दन्तः केशिनः अग्निर्वायुः सूर्य्यश्च एते त्रयः स्तूयन्ते ।

मुनयो वातरशनाः पिशंगावसते मला ।
वातस्यानुध्राजि यन्ति यद्देवासो अविक्षतः ॥ (2)

उन्मदिता मौनेयेन वाताञ्ञातस्थिमावयम् ।
शरीरेदमस्माकं यूयं मर्तासो अभिपश्यथ ॥ (3)

Sāyana—उन्मदिता उन्मत्तवदाचरन्तः यद्वा उत्कृष्टं मदं हर्ष प्राप्ताः ।

अन्तरिक्षेण पतति विश्वारूपावचाकशत् ।
मुनिर्देवस्य देवस्य सौकृत्याय सखाहितः ॥ (4)

वातस्याश्वो वायोःसखाऽश्रो देवेषितो मुनिः ।
उभौ समुद्रावाक्षेति यश्च पूर्ब्ब उतापरः ॥ (5)

अपसरसां गन्धर्वानां मृगानां चरणे चरन् ।
केशी केतस्य विद्वान् सखा स्वादुर्मदिन्तमः ॥ (6)

वायुरस्मा उपामन्थत् पिनष्टि स्नाकुनंनमा ।

केशी विषस्य पात्रेण यद्रुद्रेणापिवत् सह ॥ (7)

Sāyana—केशी=सूर्य्यः ।

N.B.— It will be observed that the Muni is mentioned only in 2, 3 (*Mauneya*), 4 and 5. In the other hymns the word is *Kesi*. Macdonell and Keith, rejecting Sāyana's interpretation, take this word as descriptive of the Muni, meaning 'long-haired' (see *Index to Vedic Names,* under Muni, footnote 1). Iyenger also takes the word *Kesi* in the same sense. But I am inclined to follow Sāyana in this matter. If *Kesi* really refers to the Muni, the 7th hymn becomes nonsense; if on the other hand it is taken to mean the sun, it yields very good sense.

From the orthodox commentary of Sāyana it is difficult to determine the exact character of the Munis. But in the Aitareya Brāhmana, vi, 33; Aitasa, who is called a Muni, is a character far different from a wandering religious mendicant. The legend is told about him that he commenced to recite some meaningless *mantras* to his sons one of whom, Abhyagni, fearing for his father's sanity, stopped his mouth and thereby incurred his curse which descended from him to his progeny. The character of Aitasa answers to the words उन्मदिता मौनेयेन (X. 136, 3) of which the first alternative interpretation by Sāyana is उन्मत्तवदाचरन्तः। If Aitasa is the type of the Rig-vedic Muni, he is surely not a homeless Sannyasi, Yati or Paribrajaka. The Muni described in the Upanishads however approaches more and more to the latter ideal till he is identified with the Paribrājaka.[38] But the danger of taking the later developed signification of a word to interpret its original sense is known to the merest tyro in philology. The question as to the character of the Rig vedic Muni is thus involved in great doubt: Mr. Srinivas Iyengar identifies the Rig-vedic Muni with the Sannyasin,[39] while Macdonell and Keith regard him as "more of a 'medicine man' (a character well-known among savage tribes) than a sage"—"an ascetic of magic powers with divine afflatus."[40]

In the Atharva-Veda, xv, we have the glorified description of a roving spirit who is called a Vrātya. The Vrātya in this description is a mystic figure, "who appears at one time to be a supernatural being endowed with all the attributes of all-pervading Deity, and at another as a human wanderer in need of food and lodging." (Griffith's *Translation of the Atharva Veda,* p. 199). We quote below those expressions in Bk. xv which may be said to relate to the human attributes of the Vrātya:—

व्रात्य आसीदीयमानः । (8)

स विशोऽनुव्यचलत् । तं सभा च समितिश्च सेना च सुरा चानुव्यचलन् । (9)

तद यस्यैवं विद्वान् व्रात्यो राज्ञोऽतिथिर्गृहानागच्छेत् श्रेयांसमनमात्मनो मानयेत् तथा क्षत्राय ना वृश्चते तथा राष्ट्राय न वृश्चते । (10)

तद यस्यैवं विद्वान् व्रात्योऽतिथिर्गृहानागच्छेत् स्वयमेनमभ्युदेत्य ब्रूयाद व्रात्यक्व वात्सी व्रात्योदकं व्रात्य तर्पयन्तु व्रात्य यथा ते प्रियं तथास्तु व्रात्य यथा ते वशस्तथास्तु व्रात्य यथा ते निकामस्तथास्तु । (11)

तद यस्यैवं विद्वान् व्रात्य उद्धृतेष्वग्निष्वधिश्रितेऽग्निहोत्रे अतिथिर्गृहानागच्छेत् । स्वयमेनमभ्युदेत्य ब्रूयाद व्रात्यातिसृज होष्यामीति । स चातिसृजेज्जुहुयान्नचातिसृजेन्नजुहुयात् । (12)

तद यस्यैवं विद्वान् व्रात्य एकां रात्रिमतिथिर्गृहि वसति ये पृथिव्यां पुण्यालोकास्तान तेनावरुन्धे । (13)

N.B.— The following attributes of the Vrātya are mentioned here:

(*a*) He wanders about.

(*b*) He goes among the people and is extremely popular and held in high regard.

(*c*) He is honoured by the king when he comes as a guest to his house.

(*d*) When he is a guest with a fire-worshipper, it is with his permission that sacrificial oblations should be made.

Except the expression we have extracted above, the rest of the book is devoted to a grotesque idealisation of the Vrātya.

From this description it has been inferred by Roth (in *St. Petersburg Dictionary*) that the Vrātya idealised in the Atharva-Veda is a Paribrajaka. But this identification rests on very slender basis and there is nothing in the description, except the fact that he wanders about and is honoured both by the king and the people when he becomes their guest, which lends colour to Roth's interpretation. Besides as pointed out by Macdonell and Keith,[41] Roth's identification is not borne out by other passages descriptive of the Vrātya. It is beside our purpose to enter here into the much vexed question as to whether the Vrātya is a non-Aryan or an Aryanised non-Aryan or a degenerate Aryan. But the Vrātya in Bk. xv of the Atharva-veda can by no means be called a Paribrajaka.

Except the two passages, quoted above from the Rig-veda and the Atharva-veda respectively, I do not know of any other passage suggesting the existence of the Paribrajaka in that age which has been called by Iyenger "the age of the Mantras." The condition of the Brahmacārin being the origin of that of the Paribrajaka may be left out of the question, for although the Brahmacārin is sometimes described as "roaming as far as the land of the Madras," it is always in search of a teacher or in order to learn sacrifices.[42] The Brahmacārin is a pupil and learner, while the Paribrajaka is a wandering religious man, a teacher and sage. The later Āsrama theory keeps these two conditions of life clearly apart. The Vedic hymns, therefore, which may be said to constitute the earliest and purest Aryan elements in Indian culture, do not mention clearly the condition of the religious mendicant. Now, among the non-Indian branches of the Indo-Europeans, although institutions analogous to Brahmanism are found, we do not find any trace of the existence of religious mendicancy in the earliest monuments of their literature. The Druids of Britain; the Brehons of Ireland, the Pontiffs of Rome and the Magi of Persia strongly resemble the Brahmanas of Aryan India.[43] But except in India, we do not know of the existence of Sramanism in primitive times in any country occupied by the Aryan race. The Macedonians who accompanied Alexander were struck with wonder at the Indian Gymnosophists. If they had seen anything similar to it in the Hellenic world, they would have surely made at least a passing reference to it in their lengthy accounts of the Gymnosophists.

References to the religious mendicant are found in Brahmanical literature after the 'Mantra period' (*e.g.*, Panini,[44] Brihadāranyakopanishad,[45] etc.), but the recognition of religious mendicancy as an institution of Aryan Brahmanical society seems to have been somewhat later.[46] This is proved by the gradual development of Āsrama theory in the Upanishads. The earlier Upanishads like the *Cchāndagya* and *Brihadāranyaka* do not recognise the condition of religious mendicancy as the Fourth Stage of a man's life, but they assume rather only three stages, and as Deussen has point out, it is to the later period of the Dharmasūtras and the Dharmasāstras that the fully developed theory of the Four Āsramas belongs. It may be legitimately assumed that if religious mendicancy had been an institution as old as the Mantras, it would have found recognition in the earliest Upanishads. The greater likelihood is that it was not a primitive institution of Aryan Brahmanical society, although the religious mendicant existed in India and was held in great regard. It seems therefore perfectly reasonable to think that the condition of religious mendicancy developed on the Indian soil and was not introduced into the country by the early Aryan settlers whose life and society are reflected to us from the Vedic Mantras.

It may be taken for granted that the Brahmanical Dharmasāstras, although they betray the intrusion into them of diverse cultural elements, carry on the traditions of ancient Aryan life and society in those ideals which they consistently approve and exalt. Now, from the Cchāndogyopanishad down to the latest Samhitās, we observe the preference, consistently held, for the house holder's state, the Second Āsrama. All the passages bearing on this point are cited in the *Appendix* to this chapter. The Upanishad doctrine of 'Emancipation through knowledge of Ātman' seems to have enfeebled only for a time the emphasis in Brahmanism on house-hold life, by bringing to the foreground the idea of Nyāsa. Otherwise the Second Āsrama is extolled and exalted, regarded as the root and mainstay of the others, and for salvation, it is said, one need not go further. Other conditions of life which tend to prevent or postpone it, *e.g.*, persistence in Brahmacarya, etc., are deliberately ruled out.[47] The striking contrast that these passages offer to the Buddhist and Jaina ideas on household life is eminently suggestive—a contrast which is well illustrated by the place and importance of the *Grihya Sūtras* in Brahmanism, the nidus out of which the whole Ācāra of the later Smritis has sprung, and the insignificant place held by the *Gahapati Vaggas* in Buddhism.[48] Over against the two dubious passages of the Rig-veda and the Atharva-veda, we may cite the whole trend of Brahmanical literature (with the exception of some of the later Upanishads) to show that Aryan life and society did not favour religious mendicancy. What is more interesting,—the rooted antagonism to it, though never clearly professed, comes out in many curious forms—in the idea for instance that the presence of a Munda is inauspicious and vitiates sacred rites. This belief is not due to any lately developed anti-Buddhistic bias, for we find an instance of it even in the Sutta-nipāta. In Vasala Sutta, the Brahmana Aggika Bharadvāja is engaged in sacrificing to the fire when he observes Buddha approaching him and calls out to him in anger to stay where he is—Tatr'eva mundaka tatr'eva samanaka tatr'eva vasakala titthahīti.[49] More than fifteen hundred years after, the same spirit dictates Mandana Misra when he rails at Sankara for intruding on his sacrificial oblations, although Sankara is a Brahmana Sannyasin—

तदानीं मण्डनमिश्रो विश्वेदेवान् सङ्कल्पा शालग्राम स्वागतमिति दर्भाक्षतप्रक्षणकाले शङ्कराचार्य्यपादद्वयं मण्डलस्थं ददर्श । ततः सर्ब्बाङ्गानि वोक्ष्य क्षणेन किलायं संत्रयासीति ज्ञात्वा कोपकोलाहलचित्तः कुतो मुण्डीत्ववादीत् । इति प्रथमवाक्यं मिश्रस्य ।[50]

If the mystic figure in Book XV of the Atharva-veda is really a Paribrajaka, it is significant that he is only a Vrātya and not a genuine or out and-out Aryan.

Another highly significant point to be noticed is that one who wishes to embrace the life of a religious mendicant has to discard all the marks of Aryan birth and breeding, *e.g.*,

तं होवाच प्रजापतिस्तव पुत्रांन् भ्रातहन् वन्ध्वादींश्छिखां यज्ञोपवीतञ्च यागञ्च सूत्रञ्च स्वाध्यायञ्च भूर्लोकभुवलोकस्वर्लोकमिहलोकजनलोकतपोलोकसत्यलोकञ्च अतलपातालवितल-सुतलरसातलमहात-लतलातलं ब्रह्माण्डञ्चविसर्जयेत् दण्डमाच्छादनञ्च परिग्रहेत्। शेष विसृजेत् ।[51]

Now the factum of this rejection of the distinctive marks of Aryan birth, breeding and culture is glozed over in the Upanishads by fanciful interpretations. The Sannyasi does not offer याग but still he may be said to be doing प्राणाग्निहोत्र;[52] "the sacrificial fire he takes up into the fire of his belly; the Gāyatri into the fire of his Speech"; the यज्ञोपवीत and शिखा, the twin symbols of Aryan ritualism, are discarded indeed, but "henceforth meditation alone is to serve as sacrificial cord and knowledge as the lock of hair—timeless Ātman is to be both sacred thread and 'lock of hair' for him who has renounced the world."[53] Observe the attempt made in these passages to Aryanise, as it were, the Sannyasin,—to show that although he has outwardly discarded the marks and symbols of Aryan culture, he still retains them in mind and spirit, possessing indeed all these signs, though it be in a spiritual sense. The glosses were necessary because the anomaly of recommending a somewhat, non-Aryan mode of life was felt. Further, that this mode of life implies a definite break with the Vedas and the culture based on their authority seems to be implied in some of the preliminaries, recommended in the Upanishads, to be gone through by an intending Sannyasin. One of these is a simple offering to fire or water (Jāvāla, 4) with the words—ॐ सर्ब्बाभ्यो देवताभ्यो जुहोमि स्वाहेति । Here, ॐ, it is said, implies the three Vedas (मोक्षमन्त्रस्त्रय्येवं विन्देत्—*ibid*). Perhaps it signifies that the Vedas are first to be sacrificed to the Gods by the intending Sannyasin.

In conclusion we must note the fact that the position of the Sramana was regarded by the people as being on a level of equality with the Brahmana: yet the Sramana is sharply distinguished from the latter,—and the Greek accounts, which have an inestimable value as being based on the observation, however defective, of real life unbiased by theories, bear ample testimony to the fact that between these two classes there was a spirit of rivalry and competition.[54] The expression *Sramana-Brāhmanam* is taken by Patanjali in illustration of the rule येषाञ्च विरोधः शाश्वतिकः,[55] and the word, Sramana, in the expression need not necessarily be taken in the sense of a Buddhist Bhikkhu, for a Sramana might possibly mean even a Brahmanical Paribrajaka or Sannyasi.[56] How the casteless Sramanas,[57] not recognising the authority of the Vedas,[58] attacking the superiority of the Brahmanas,[59] sharply distinguished from them, attained an equal level with the highest caste of Aryan society in India appears like a standing puzzle. The result could not possibly have been brought about by the inner forces of Aryan society itself in which so far as we can trace the Brahmana class occupies the highest and most honourable place, though a trace of Kshatriya antagonism to their superiority appears in the Upanishads as well as in Jaina and Buddhist literature. The clue is probably to be found in the fact that the culture which is represented by Vedic literature and its derivatives was only one strand—it might be the predominant one—in the highly mixed warp and woof of ancient Indian life and civilization.

Since the time of Max Müller and 'the Philologists' the theory of the Aryan occupation of Indian has been considerably modified by researches into Indian ethnology and sociology. The theory is being gradually narrowed to the conclusion that the Aryans (whether they came in one immigration or more) were "a small body of foreign immigrants," who, without producing great racial disturbances, acted as a strong leaven in the vast population of Dravidian and Munda races that occupied India.[60] The rich and virile culture of this small minority slowly infiltrated the life and civilization of the native non-Aryan populations till even their Aryan language was adoted by the natives in whose mouths it broke up into various dialects, in the same manner as rustic Latin fermented into the Romance Languages in Southern Europe. The process of the Aryanisation of northern India was not the forced super-imposition but the gradual infiltration of a dominant culture which slowly but surely settled into a distinct Indian type. This process, having started from its original source in a definitely circumscribed circle of peoples in the West, seems to have gradually advanced towards the East along the valley of the Ganges. The Brāhmana literature points indeed to this circle of peoples as the radiating centre of Aryan culture; they correspond with those who are celebrated by Manu as upright in life; and they go back to the most prominent Aryan stocks mentioned in the Rig-Veda.[61] The Aryans and the Aryanised succeeded in assimilating to themselves large bodies of native population, converting them to their cult,[62] taking them as serfs or slaves, or elevating them to a recognised social standing by such ceremonies as the *Vrātya-stomas* described in the Pancavimsa-Brāhmana.[63] We cannot trace the successive stages of this eastward progress of Aryanisation, but the antique legend in the Satapatha-Brāhmana of the progress of Agni Vaiswanara marks a stage at which the Aryan influence stopped at the 'sundering stream' of Sadānīrā, near the confluence of the Ganges and the Jamuna. The legend of the Satapatha-Brāhmana may be safely taken to be much older than the rise of Buddhism and Jainism. Beyond the confluence of the Ganges and the Jamuna are located many of the most prominent tribes and clans mentioned in Pali literature—Vacchas, Cetis, Mallas, Vijjis, Licchavis, Videhas, Kosalas, Kasis, Sakyas, Magadhas and Angas.[64] Three of the eastern tribes *viz.*, Bangas, Magadhas (Bagadhas?) and Ceras are, curiously enough, referred to in the Aitareya Āranyaka as species of birds.[65] These tribes and clans seem to have been out of the pale of the Aryan communities, but between the time of the Satapatha legend and the rise of Buddhism and Jainism, they must have been strongly leavened with Aryan thought and civilization. The conclusions formulated above are however still of a somewhat hypothetical character, but it is not possible for us within the limits of the present thesis to deal exhaustively with all the arguments that may be adduced in support of them—arguments turning on various aspects of Indian proto-history and pre-history.

But if we make the perfectly legitimate presumption that from age to age a process of Aryanisation was going on in northern Indian before the rise of buddhism, profoundly influencing tribe after tribe and clan after clan, we have to observe further that the Aryan leaven must have worked in two converging lines—(*i*) in the spread of Aryan thoughts, ideas and beliefs, and (*ii*) in the much slower process of the modification and replacement of non-Aryan institutions by the Aryan. We know how rapidly mind influences mind and how slowly the settled habits of social life are changed and modified. Historical instances may be taken at random from almost anywhere—even from modern India itself under European influence. The process of Aryanisation on the mere intellectual side must have gone on in the east at a more rapid rate than that in social customs and institutions, and from this fact most interesting results would emerge. The divergence between the twofold process of Aryanisation, on the intellectual side and the social, would tend to increase more and more, as we receded further and further east from the homeland of Aryan culture, the Āryāvarta, and the result of this divergence would naturally be more palpable and pronounced at the eastern borderland of Aryan civilization, exactly where in the 6th century B.C. Buddhism and Jainism arose.

Now the distinctive mental culture of the Aryans had, by the 8th and 7th centuries, various means of conservation, 'various modes of expression. First, there was the priestly class, the Brahmanas, the repositories of traditional learning, by whom philosophic speculations were carried on and developed. Secondly, there were the clannish academies like the Parishad of the Pancālas to which Svetaketu, in the Brihadāranyakopanishad, went for instruction.[66] Thirdly, there were the domestic centres of learning, the residences of Ācaryas, Upādhyāyas and Gurus. Fourthly, there was at least one University of Asiatic fame that flourished at Takkasila with the traditions of which the Buddhist Jatakas are replete. Did analogous institutions exist among the peoples of the east—the non-Aryan or imperfectly Aryanised tribes and clans?

If the answer be in the negative, it is reasonable to suppose that when Aryan thought and culture invaded their society, it was diffused and dispersed among the populace. Who among them would be professors of the new learning? There were probably no Brahmanas in their social economy, no class of men who were traditionary repositories of learning. Nor could this new learning produce among them complete systems of philosophy, as they had probably no conservative and corporate centres of learning,—academies or universities,—where speculative ideas are moulded into philosophic systems. The impact of Aryan thoughts, ideas, speculations of philosophy on the imperfectly Aryanised communities, without the characteristic Aryan institutions, seem to have given birth, even some three centuries before the birth of Buddhism (if an approximate chronology were needed), to this class of men, answering to the Brahmanas in Aryan society, who went about in a missionary spirit, dealing in philosophic speculations, teaching the uninstructed, and gaining honour and reputation thereby wherever they went. They were really the torch-bearers of a new Aryan learning like the *Scholastici Vagantes* of Renaissance Europe. This, it seems to me, to have been the true origin of the Sramanas. Even in the 6th century, B.C. they were much more in evidence in the eastern regions, for reasons suggested above, and they therefore occupy a more distinguished place in the literature that originated in the east—in the Buddhist Pitakas and the Jaina Angas. "It is in the East," says an ancient Buddhist tradition, "that the Buddhas are born."[67]

If this theory of the origin of the Sramana institution be accepted, it helps us a good deal in understanding several points about the Sramanas. The Sramana is a religious teacher, seeking convertities; he wanders about, most likely because the institution of the residential teacher is not established among the imperfectly Aryanised communities; his speculations are fragmentary and unsystematic as, in the absence of such consolidating agencies as academies and universities, we may naturally expect them to be; he is honoured as much as the Brahmanas because his function with regard to society is the same, namely, to instruct; he is a more important personage in the literature which reflects the life and society of the east more than that of the west, and lastly we must read the significance of the most striking feature of his character, his extreme earnestness, betokening the zeal of the professor of a comparatively new learning. The institution of Sramanism seems thus to have grown up among the imperfectly Aryanised communities of the east, spread, flourished and become highly popular, and with the remarkable elasticity which is characteristic of Brahmanism, it was later off affiliated to the Aryan system and theory of life, becoming the Fourth Āsrama. Along the upper reaches of the Ganges, where we find residential teachers, clannish academies and the Brahmana class, the place and function of the wandering philosophers was neither noteworthy nor important,—hence their scanty recognition in Brahmanical literature. But lower down they grew in number and importance and their religio-intellectual activities affected more deeply and widely the life of the people. Hence their abundance and pre-eminence in Buddhist and Jaina literature that had grown up in the east.

References

1. Steinthal's *Udānam* (P.T.S), pp. 66-67.
2. See Chapter V of the present thesis.
3. See the description of the practices of the Samanas and Brahmanas in *Kassapasihanada-sutta* in Digha Nikaya. There was at first no clear line of division between the Vanaprastha or Tāpasa and the Sannyasin.—See Deussen's *Upanishads,* p. 372.
4. See *Jaina Sutras* (S.B.E.), Pt. II, pp. 405-409.
5. See *Kassapa-sihanada-sutta*, 21 (D.N.—P.T.S., Vol. I, p. 174).
6. See *Samanna-phala-sutta,* 14,—Samana-brahmanesu uddhaggikam dakkhinam patitthapenti sovaggikam sukha-vipakam sagga-samvattanika.
7. See *Jaina Sutras,* Pt. II, p. 39—In the *Pravrajya of King Nami,* Sakra in the guise of a Brahmana tries to dissuade King Nami from the life of the Sramana and calls upon him to assume his kingly duties at Mithila. Among other things, Sakra says, "Offer great sacrifices, *feed Svamanas and Brahmanas*, give alms, enjoy yourself and offer sacrifices: thus you will be a true Kshattriya."
8. On auspicious days many Sramanas and Brahmanas, guests, paupers and beggars are entertained with food—*Jaina Sutras*, Pt. I, p. 92.
9. See *Girnir Inscriptions, Sahabajgar Inscriptions,* etc.
10. *E.g.*, अष्टश्रमखा ब्राह्मणा अष्ट जनपदेषु क्षत्रिया ।
    अष्ट स इन्द्रका देवा सदा रक्षां करोन्तु वः ॥
    Senart's *Mahāvastu*, III, 310, 5.
11. See *Sutrakritānga* (*Jaina Sutras,* pt. II, pp. 339 ff).
12. See *Samanna-phala-sutta,* 35, 36.
13. See *Madhurā Sutta* in Majjhima Nikaya (J.R.A.S., 1894, p. 356, Text and Translation by Robert Chalmers.)
14. See for example the opening sections of *Samanna-phala Sutta.*
15. Rhys Davids says (*Dialogues of the Buddha,*Vol. II, p. 103): "We have seen how in the Sāmanna-phala-Sutta, it is taken for granted that a slave would join an Order (that is any Order, not the Buddhist?). And in he Aganna Sutta of the Digha and the Madhurā Sutta of the Majjhima, there is

express mention of the Sudras becoming Samanas *as if it were a recognised and common occurrence long before the time of the rise of Buddhism*. So in the Jataka (III, 381) we hear of a potter, and at IV, 392 of a Candala, who became Samanas (not Buddhist Samanas)."

16. *C.f.* Tena kho pana Nigrodha paribbajako samayena Udambarikaya paribbajakarame pativasati mahatiya paribbajakaparisaya saddhim timsa-mattehi paribbajaka-satehi—*Udumbarika sihanada-suttanta* (Digha Nikaya, P.T.S., III, p. 36).
17. See Chapter II, of the present thesis.
18. See Mahavagga, I, 22.
19. See Chapter III, footnote 1.
20. *Buddhist India,* pp. 144-46; *Dialogues of Buddha,* II, pp. 220-222.
21. See Tenckner's *Milindapanho,* p. 191.
22. See *Jaina Sutras,* Pt. I, p. 128, footnote 1.
23. See the Cave Dedications of Dasaratha in the Nāgārjuni Hills—Smith's *Asoka*, p. 201.
24. See *Buddhist India,* p. 142. See also *Potthapada Sutta,* 1 (Digha Nikaya, P.T.S., Vol. I, p. 178).
25. See *Jaina Sutras,* Pt. II, Intro. pp. xxxi-xxxii.
26. See *Uvāsagadasāo* (Bibliotheca Indica), pp. 108-111 (footnote, 253).
27. See *ibid.* The story of Mahavira's discipleship of and subsequent breach with Gosāla is told in *Bhagavati Sutta.* The passage is translated by Hoernle: *Uvā.*, Appendix.
28. The name 'Sramana' is not usually applied to a Brahmanical Paribrajaka in the Dharmasutras and Dharmasastras. Medhatithi however refers to a *Sramanaka Sutra* as an authority on certain practices of the Hindu Paribrajaka in his commentary on Manu, VI, 25. (See Bühler's *Laws of Manu*, S.B.E., p. 203, Note).
29. See Oman's *The Mystics, Ascetics and Saints of India* (Ch. VI on *Sadhus as described by some European Visitors to India*).
30. *Buddhist India,* p. 159.
31. "Then suddenly and almost simultaneously, and almost certainly independently, there is evidence, about the sixth century, B.C., in each of these widely separated centres of civilization (China, Persia, Egypt, Italy, Greece), of a leap forward in speculative thought, of a new birth in ethics, of a religion of conscience threatening to take the place of the old religion of custom and magic."—*Buddhist India,* p. 239.
32. See Deussen's *The Upanisads,* pp. 361, ff.
33. The following is Deussen's argument (*ibid.*, p. 411-12):—"The clothing of the doctrine of emancipation in empirical forms involved as a consequence the conceiving of emancipation, as though it were an event in an empirical sense, from the point of view of causality, as an effect that might be brought

about or accelerated by appropriate means. Now emancipation consisted in its external phenomenal side:—

(*i*) In the removal of the consciousness of plurality.

(*ii*) In the removal of all desire, the necessary consequence and accompaniment of that consciousness.

"To produce these two states artificially was the aim of two characteristic manifestations of Indian culture:

(*i*) Of the 'Yoga', which by withdrawing the organs from the objects of sense and concentrating them on the inner self endeavoured to shake itself free from the world of plurality and to secure union with the 'Atma.'

(*ii*) Of the 'Sannyāsa,' which by casting off from oneself of home, possessions, family, and all that stimultes desire seeks laboriously to realise that freedom from all the ties of the earth."

(The passage is somewhat abridged.)

34. See Ch. II of the present thesis, footnote 4.

35. *E.g.*, Sambādho gharāvāso rajo-patho abbhokās pabbajjā. Naidam sukaram agāram ajjhāvasatā ekantaparipunnam ekantaparisuddham sankha-likhitam brahmacariyam caritum—See *Samauna-phala-sutta,* V, 41 (D.N., P.T.S., Vol. I, p. 63). This passage is repeated in *Tevigga Sutta*. See also *Muni Sutta,* 14, 15, in Sutta-nipata (*Buddhist Suttas,* S.B.E., pp. 35-36).

36. See Kingsley's *Hypatia.*

37. See Oldenberg's *The Buddha,* pp. 63-64 (Hoey's Translation).

38. The fourth Āsrama is called by Āpastamba that of Mauna.

Cf. Dhammapada (Fausböll, no. 49)

Yathapi bhamaro puppham vanna gandham ahethayam

Paleti rasamādāya evam gāme muni care.

This is the description of Paribrajaka—a character different from one who is "maddened with divine afflatus" (unmaditā mauneyena). Here the Muni and the Paribrajaka are completely identified.

39. See Iyengar's *Life in Ancient India in the Age of the Mantras,* p. 77—"As Brahmacaryam, studentship, the first of the stages in the life of a Brahman, was invented in the age of the Mantras, so too, the fourth and last stage, that of the Sannyasi, called Muni, in the hymns."

40. See Macdonell and Keith's *Index to Vedic Names, Loc. cit.*

41. See Index to Vedic Names under Vrātya.

42. See *Index to Vedic Names* under Brahmacarya; also Deussen's *The Upanishads,* p. 370.

43. Dr. N.C. Sen-Gupta in his *Sources of Law and Society in Ancient India,* (Calcutta University Publication) pp.15, ff. has dealt with this point.

44. Panini mentions '*Bhikkhu Sutra*' in IV, 3, 100.

पाराशर्य शिलालिभ्यां भिक्षुनटयूत्रवीः ।

45. See *Brihadāranyaka*, IV, 3.22—श्रमणोऽश्रमणस्तापसोऽस्तापसः ।

46. This has been clearly pointed out by Deussen. His arguments and authorities will be found at pp. 367-369 of *The Upanishads*.

47. "दीर्घकालं ब्रह्मचर्य्यं, *etc.*, एतानि लोकगुप्तार्थं कलेरादौ महात्मभिः । निवर्त्तितानि कर्म्माणि व्यवस्थापूर्व्वकं बुधैः"—पराशरभाष्यधृतमादिपुराणम् ।

In *Vrihan-Nāradiya-Purana*, xxii, 12-16, among practices avoidable in the Kaliyuga, though permitted by the sacred books, are mentioned वाणप्रस्थाश्रमः and दीर्घकालं ब्रह्मचर्य्यं । Vide also कृष्णद्वैपायनस्य गृहीतनैष्ठिकब्रह्मचर्य्यस्य, etc., etc... per Kumarila Bhatta, quoted in Max Müller's *History of Ancient Sanskrit Literature*, (Panini Office Ed.), p. 25, foot-note 3.

48. It will be observed that the *Gahapati Vaggas* lack any distinctive Buddhist character. Sometimes, as Kern has pointed out (*Man. of Ind. Bud.*, p. 68), they are borrowed from the Brahmancial scriptures and are at variance with Buddhistic doctrines. Kern observes that Buddhism is properly a monastic institution, and the laity is but accessory (*ibid*, p. 72). Dr. Archibald Scott finds the broadest distinction between the Christian Church and the Buddhist Church in the fact that the work of the former lay outside the limits of the Church. Of Buddhism, he says, "Its lay associates, however numerous were but the fringes of religious communities. When, therefore, deterioration in the Order set in, reformation of it by the people was hopeless." (*Buddhism and Christianity*, p. 272).

49. See Fausböll's *Sutta*-Nipāta, P.T.S., p. 21.

50. See Anandagiri's *Sankara-Vijaya* (Jivananda Vidyasagar's Ed., p. 284).

51. See *Āruneyopanishad*, I.

52. See Deussen on *Prānāgnihotra* (*The Upanishads*, pp. 124 ff.).

53. See Deussen's *The Upanishads*, pp. 376, 377, where all the authorities are referred to.

54. See Chapter V of the present thesis (Kleitarchos quoted by Strabo).

55. See *Mahābhāsya*, loc. cit.

56. See footnote, 27 of this Chapter.

57. See *Madhurā-Sutta* of Majjhima Nikaya and elsewhere to the effect that all castes are merged in the life of Sramana.

58. See *Tevijja Sutta* of Digha Nikaya (D.N., Vol. I) and elsewhere in the Suttapitaka.

59. See *Ambattha Sutta* in Digha Nikaya (see also Rhys Davids' *The Dialogues of the Buddha*, Vol. II, pp. 103 ff); *Madhurā Sutta* in *ibid*; see also the famous comparison of Buddhist *Dhamma-Vinaya* to the ocean having 8 qualities in which the four castes are likened to four rivers which lose themselves in the ocean (Culla, IX, 1, 4). Similar ideas are found elsewhere in Buddhist literature. In the Jaina *Kalpa-Sutra* (in Bhadravahu's *Lives of the Ginas*), it is said that Arhats, etc., are not born in low families, mean families, degraded families, poor families, indigent families, beggar's families or Brahmanical families. (Jai, Su, 1, p. 225).

60. See Oppert's *The Original Inhabitants of Bharatvarsa* and Iyengar's *Life in Ancient India.*
61. See Oldenberg's *The Buddha,* Excursus I.
62. Ragozin in his *Vedic India* (Story of the Nations Series) has hazarded the conjecture that the *Gāyatri Mantra* was the formula of conversion of the non-Aryans by the Aryan priests.
63. See Macdonnel and Keith's *Index to Vedic Names* under Vrātya.
64. A list of these tribes and clans occurs in *Buddhist India*, p. 23.
65. Ai. Ār. 11, 1, 1.—*But the expression is of doubtful import and cannot be insisted on.*
66. श्वेतकेतुर्ह वा आरुणेया पञ्चालानां परिषदमाजगाम ।—VI. 2-1.

    It appears from this reference that the Parishad was an academic institution attached to a clan, to which learners after the completion of preliminary studies used to resort. The descendants of the Vedic Parishads may be traced on the one hand to the King's *Sabhā,* mentioned by Manu, VIII. 1; Jajnavalkya, II, 1, *ets eq.*, Narada, I, 15, etc., and on the other hand to the *Parishads* mentioned by Vasistha, III, 20; Gautama, XXVIII, 49 and other Smriti writers.
67. See Cullavagga, XII, 2, 3.

Appendix

Chapter II

(The Exaltation of the Second Āsrama in Brāhmanical Literature See p. 53)

Literature See p. 53

I

(*Cchāndagyopanishad, VIII, 15*)

तद्धैद ब्रह्मा प्रजापत उवाच प्रजातिर्मनवे मनुः प्रजाभ्यः आचार्य्यकुलाद वेदमधीत्य यथाविधानं गुरोः कर्म्मातिशेषेणाभिसमाकृत्य कुटम्वे शुचौ देशे स्वाध्यायमधीयानो धार्म्मिकान् विदधदात्मनि सर्ब्बेन्द्रियाणि सप्रतिष्ठाप्याहिंसन् सर्व्वभूतान्यन्यत्र तीर्थेभ्यः स खल्वेवं वर्त्तयन् यावदांयुषं ब्रह्मलोकमभिसम्पद्यते न च पुनरावर्त्तते न च पुनरावर्त्तते।

II

(*Gautama, Ch. III*)

ब्रह्मचारी गृहस्थो भिक्षुर्वैखानस इति तेषां गृहस्थो योनिरप्रजनत्वादितरेषाम् ।

III

(*Manu, Ch. III, 77-80; ibid., Ch. VI. 87, 89, 90*)

यथा वायु समाश्रित्य वर्त्तन्ते सर्व्वजन्तवः ।

तथा गृहस्थमाश्रित्य वर्त्तन्ते सर्ब्ब आश्रमाः ॥

यस्मात् त्रयोऽप्याश्रमिणो ज्ञानेनान्नेनचान्वहम् ।

गृहस्थेनैव धार्य्यन्ते तस्माज्ज्येष्ठाश्रमो गृही ॥ *et. seq.*

IV

(*Vasistha, Ch. III*)

गृहस्थ एव यजते गृहस्थस्तप्यते तपः ।

चतुर्णामाश्रमानान्तु गृहस्थस्तुं विशिष्यते ॥

यथा नदीनदाः सर्ब्बे समुद्रे यान्ति संस्थितिम् ।

एवमाश्रमिणः सर्ब्बे गृहस्थे यान्ति संस्थितिम् ॥
यथा भातरमाश्रित्य सर्ब्बे जीवन्ति जंन्तवः।
एवं गृहस्थमाश्रित्य सर्ब्बे जीवन्ति भिक्षुकाः ॥ *et. seq.*

V

(*Sankha, Ch. V, 5, 6*)

वाणप्रस्थो ब्रह्मचारी यतिश्चैव तथाद्विजः ।
गृहस्थस्य प्रसादेन जीवन्त्येते यथाविधि ॥
गृहस्थ एव यजते गृहस्थस्तप्यते तपः ।
दाताचैव गृहस्थः स्यात् तस्माज्ज्येष्ठो गृहाश्रमी ॥

VI

(*Vasistha, Ch. VIII—Cchāndagya., 8,15*)

नित्योदकी नित्ययज्ञोपवीती ।
नित्यस्वाध्यायी पतितान्नवर्जी ॥
ऋतौगच्छन् विधिवच्चजुह्वन् ।
न ब्राह्मणश्चव्यते ब्रह्मलोकात् ॥

VII

(*Visnu, Ch. LIX, 28, 29*)

गृहस्थ एव यजते गृहस्थस्तप्यते तपः ।
ददाति च गृहस्थस्तु तस्माज्ज्येष्ठो गृहाश्रमी ॥
ऋषयः पितरो देवा भूतान्यतिथयस्तथा ।
आशासते कुटुम्बिभ्यस्तस्माज्ज्येष्ठो गृहाश्रमी ॥

VIII

(*Vyāsa, Ch. IV, 2*)

गृहाश्रमात् परो धर्म्म नास्ति नास्ति पुनः पुनः।
सर्ब्बतीर्थफलं तस्य यथोक्तं यस्तु पालयेत् ॥

3

The Sangha and the Pātimokkha : Development of the Latter

The Paribrājaka, by the necessity of his manner of life, had to live outside the pale of organised society: he was absolved from all social and domestic ties. But even for a professed recluse and solitary the deep-seated gregarious instinct of man is difficult to abjure. Thus among the primitive Paribrājakas, sects and parties appear to have abounded. We find Sanghas and Ganas among them each recognising the leadership of a spiritual head. The famous story of Sanjaya in Mahavagga, I, 23, in an illustration in point. Sanjaya was at the head of two hundred and fifty Paribrajakas and among them, two who were afterwards destined to be the foremost of Buddha's disciples, Sāriputta and Moggallāna. When these two communicated to Sanjaya their desire of transferring their spiritual allegiance to Buddha, Sanjaya offered to divide the leadership of the Gana with them—Sabbeva tayo imam ganam pariharissāmā ti. In the same story the relation between a Paribrajaka leader, called elsewhere a Ganācariyo, and his body of followers is set out in the following dialogue between Sāriputta and Assaji. Sāriputta asks: Kam si tvam āvuso uddissa pabbajito, ko vā te satthā, kassa vā tvam dhammam rocesīti? (The same question, it will be observed, is put by Upaka to Buddha in Mahavagga, I, 6.7). Assaji answers: Atth' avuso mahāsamano sakyaputto sakyakulā pabbajito, tāham bhagavantam uddissa pabbajito, so ca me bhagavā satthā, tassa cāham bhagavato dhammam recemīti. Sāriputta next puts the question: Kimbādī panāyasmato satthā. Kimakkā yīti. To which Assaji replies: Aham kho āvuso navo acirapabbajito adhunāgato imam dhammavinayam na t'āham sakkomi vitthārena dhammam desetum, api ca te samkhittena attham vakkhāmīti. This brief conversation between Sariputta and Assaji is highly significant. Among the Paribrajakas, it appears from this, there were founders and leaders of sects, who had organised bodies of followers recognising their headship. Six of them are frequently referred to in the Pali books as 'sanghī ganī ganācariyao.'[1] One who had left the household state would often be a convert to a sect-leader, a Ganācariyo (uddissa pabbajito) recognising him as his master (Satthā) and accepting his doctrines (Dhammam). He would thereby be admitted to the membership of a certain Gana or Sangha, though he would be free to back out of it and affiliate himself to another.[2] The Brahmanical books however in the rules which they lay down for the regulation of the Paribrājaka contain no allusion to such associations among the Paribrājakas. Rhys Davids however finds some obscure indications of the existence of associations of this kind among the Brahmanical Paribrājakas too.[3] It is curious to observe how in the fourth Āsrama there grew up a type of association resembling the association of a teacher and his pupils as in the first Āsrama, and in Pali literature the relation between a Satthā and his followers is often and often indicated by the word, Brahmacariya.[4] Like the other great teachers of his time, Buddha was the founder of a sect of Paribrajakas. Many religious mendicants were initiated into this sect, recognising Buddha as their Satthā and accepting his Dhamma. The Pali scriptures represent him as being accompanied in his peregrinations with a great multitude of followers (mahatā bhikkhusanghena saddham) and this body of Buddha's followers came to be known as Cātuddiso Bhikkhusangho, the significance of which phrase we shall examine later on.

In the Vinayapitaka the followers of Buddha are also called Sakyaputta-Samanas. Buddha himself is frequently called Sakyaputta. But in what relation Buddha stood to the Sakyaputta-Samanas, the original body of his followers, is somewhat difficult to make out. We are confronted with the inevitable question, whether the Sakyaputta-Samanas constituted a mere *Sect*,[5] a gana or sangha (in its original sense), or an *Order.*[6] In other words, the question is—Was there merely a community of faith and belief among them or was there any *external* bond of union, *e.g.*, a distinguishing sign, common observance of distinctive rites, any special code of conduct, etc.? The distinction between a Sect and an Order is of the broadest and the loose use of these two terms has often led to a confusion of ideas as regards the true character of the original body of Buddha's followers.

The Sakyaputta-Samanas undoubtedly constituted one of the several Sanghas or Ganas into which the vast Paribrajaka community of India of 6th century, B.C. was divided. Among the Buddhist Sangha, there was no doubt the bond of a common dhamma which is represented by that body of cardinal doctrines which are repeated again and again in the Nikāyas, summed up in the Mahāparinibbāna Suttanta and included by later writers in their category of the Bodhapakkhiyā dhammā.[7] But this dhamma, that bound together the Sangha of which Buddha was the Satthā, was not mere philosophy or creed, but had a practical ethical bearing which we find clearly exhibited in Sāmannaphala Sutta and elsewhere. There were certain rules of moral conduct associated with the primitive Buddhistic faith. But what was the general character of these rules? Even a rapid review of them would leave no room for doubt that they could not be intended to serve as the distinctive rules of any religious Order. They relate to right conduct generally as understood by the Paribrājakas and one may find many of them even in St. Benedict's *Instruments of Good Works.*[8] We cannot find in these rules any distinctive Buddhistic stamp, such as strongly marks and individualises the statement of Buddhist faith in the Mahāparinibbāna Suttanta. In the primitive Buddhist community, while the Dhamma was the special dhamma of a particular Sangha, the Vinaya was not of this character; it was not the vinaya of any particular Sangha, but was of broad and general application. An episode in the Mahāparinibbāna Suttanta throws a flood of light on this point.[9] Ananda expresses to Buddha the hope—"na tāva Bhagavā parinibbāyissati na yāva Bhagavā bhikkhu-sangham ārabbha kincid eva udāharatīti." Buddha repudiates the idea saying, "Kim Ānanda Tathāgato bhikkhu-sangam ārabbha kincid eva udāharissīti," and refuses to lay down any rules for the Sangha, saying, "Tathāgatassa kho Ānanda na evam hoti aham bhikkhu-sangham parihārissamīti vā mam' uddesiko bhikkhu-sangho'ti vā,"—a curious inconsistency with what Assaji says, "tāham bhagavantam uddissa pabbajito"—an inconsistency in which we may discover the beginning of a change of character of the Buddhist Sangha.[10] Now considering this episode "in the only way in which any such record can be considered authentic, that is, as evidence of beliefs held at the date at which it was composed,"[11] the conclusion is irresistible that the idea of the primitive Buddhist community was that Buddha himself had laid down no distinctive rules for the regulation of the Sangha which must therefore have been of later growth. There may seem to be an apparent inconsistency in Buddha's saying later on in the same Suttanta, "Yo vo Ananda mayā dhammo ca vinayo ca desito, etc.,"[12] but the inconsistency vanishes if we regard 'vinayo' in the present context as not signifying the rules of an Order, but only the general rules of right conduct. We find however in the Dhammika Sutta in Suttanipāta an approach to the formulation of a distinctive body of rules designed for a particular religious Order.[13] The rules given in this Sutta do not betray the character of a redaction from the Vinayapitaka, and we find no hard and fast elaboration of details, but only broad and general rules which however apply specifically to a Buddhist Bhikkhu. The next step must have been to give a new character and authority to the rules by constituting them into the special rules of the Buddhist Order, and I am inclined to think that this step was taken at the First Buddhist Council, about the historicity (though not the date) of which no reasonable doubts can be entertained. The whole corpus of Buddhist canon law has been moulded to conform to the theory that it proceeded bodily from the lips of Buddha, which is curiously analogous to the well-known theory of the Vedic origin of Hindu law adhered to by Hindu lawyers.[14] No true historical view of either is possible unless we are prepared to lift the obscuring veil of such traditionary origins. Among the Paribrajakas of the 6th century, B.C. certain rules of right conduct such as the Sīlas were generally recognised. The condition of religious mendicancy naturally connoted certain practices and abstinences. There is no reason to suppose that the primitive Buddhist Paribrajakas did not abide by them. It seems on the other hand, as the story of Subhadda would seem to signify,[15] that Buddha himself had enjoined strictness with regard to many of them. The followers of the great Teacher obeyed these rules of Paribrajaka life as presumably the other Paribrajakas also did. But afterwards the most important of such general and universal rules of right conduct for the Paribrajakas were modified and transformed into the specific rules of a *Buddhist Order.* To take an example, we find the Cattāri Akaranīyāni (Maha., 1, 78) which are nothing but general rules of conduct involved in the acceptance of the religious life of the Paribrajaka, enacted into the four Pārājika Dhammā, becoming thereby part of the canon law of the Buddhist Order. A settlement of the Buddhist Vinaya seems to have been made in this way at the First Buddhist Council. The character of the First Council however has been much obscured by later traditions. The account of the proceedings has little historical value and no conclusion can be based upon it. Yet certain indisputable points stand out in the legendary account that we find in the 11th khandaka of the Cullavagga. In the first place, though both Dhamma and Vinaya are said to have been rehearsed here, the council is called Vinaya-Sangīti.[16] In the second place, we observe the more important place that is assigned throughout both in the statement of the reason and occasion for the holding of the Council and in the proceedings themselves to Vinaya than to Dhamma. In fact, reading the whole account between the lines, it appears clearly that though the historical story of Subhadda might not have been, as has been shown by Oldenberg,[17] the immediate occasion for the holding of the Council, it was initiated primarily for the purpose of settling what Buddha had permitted and what not. In other words, the main object of the Council was to gather up the rules of right conduct which had been mentioned by Buddha at various times, and by giving these rules an authoritative Buddhistic stamp to raise them into the special rules of a particular religious Order. In speaking therefore of the original Buddhist community we must not speak of a religious *Order*, for this implies some external bond of union other than a common dhamma. The Ganas and Sanghas among the primitive Paribrajakas of 6th century, B.C. were probably none of them religious Orders—they were simply different sects of a heterogeneous community of religious mendicants.

The primitive Buddhist Sangha in Pali literature is often called the Cātuddisa Bhikkhu-Sangha. The phrase is of pretty frequent occurrence not only in the Buddhist scriptures,[18] but also in many donatory inscriptions,[19] some of which date back to the time of Asoka. The persistency with which the expression is used in reference to the primitive Buddhist Sangha seems to indicate that it was used originally not merely as a descriptive phrase, but as a distinguishing name. In the inscriptions alluded to, the donors make endowments on a body of monks resident at a particular monastery to the use of the Sangha of the Four Quarters. In the Pali scriptures also the gift of a monastery is always made to Cātuddisa Bhikkhu-Sangha,[20] and this form of donation is adhered to in the inscriptions, though, as I shall show, in the former case the expression is the name of a real, existing body of men, in the latter it is the expression of an ideal entity. M. Senart however has given a different interpretation of the phrase, Cātuddisa Sangha, occurring in the donatory inscriptions[21] and it is necessary to examine his views. "Monastic communities," says Senart, "may be classified in two respects, *viz.*, according to their residence and according to the sect to which they belong. This double restriction is excluded in principle by the mention of Cātuddisa Sangha, though in some cases and according to the disposition of the donor, it may mean specially one or the other." He instances a Nasik cave-inscription (No. 15, 1. 7), त्रिरश्मियर्व्वतविहारवास्तव्यस्य चातुर्दिशमिक्षुसंङ्घस्य गिलानभेषजार्थम् and says that the endowments were made not for the use of the specific body of monks at a particular monastery, but for all monks from whatever quarter of the globe they might come, taking up their lodgings at that monastery during the rains. Now Senart's argument is ingenious but not convincing. The phrase, *Sangha of the Four Quarters,* had been in use long before the date of the inscriptions and long before the later Buddhist sects and separate congregational organisations had come into existence. We find it frequently in the Vinayapitaka and in Ceylonese inscriptions dating back to the time of Asoka used in contexts where no special signification of universality is intended. The phrase in fact was an historical one. Besides, the custom in later times was for monks belonging to a particular monastery to spend the Vassa in that monastery.[22] If so, the phrase in the donatory inscriptions becomes an idle one and not of any practical significance as M. Senart suggests. The real interpretation of the phrase is in fact different from that put upon it by Senart. In the lifetime of Buddha there had grown up a community of his followers, a Sangha founded by Buddha himself, who were described as the *Sangha of the Four Quarters* because they recognised no limitations of caste (as the Tedandins or Brahmanical Sannyasis did) or of locality. With the lapse of time, the original Sangha underwent divisions and subdivisions, but it began at the same time to be idealised. The Sangha of the Four Quarters meant latterly an ideal confederation which had at one time an historical reality. A Sangha in later times simply meant a body of resident monks at particular monastery, but Cātuddissa Bhikkhu-Sangha meant an ideal body, and it was to this ideal entity that donations were formally made. The two different meanings are obvious in one Nasik inscription wherein the donor gives a cave to the Sangha of the Four Quarters and gives as a perpetual endowment 100 *Kahapanas* in the hand of the Sangha (data cha nena akhayanivi kahapanasata sanghasa hathe).[23] Here the first Sangha refers to the ideal confederation of the followers of Buddha to which donations were made according to custom and form, and the second to the real Sangha, the resident body of monks, who were capable of receiving and holding property.

The idealisation of the Buddhist Sangha is a well-known phenomenon in the history of Buddhism. In the Cetokhilo Sutta, a Bhikkhu is enjoined to have faith in Satthā, Dhamma, Sangha and Sikkhā.[24] This is only a stage removed from the later creed of Buddha, Dhamma and Sangha, in which formula, Sangha must be considered as an ideal entity which may be equiparated with Buddha and Dhamma. The complete idealisation of the Sangha is to be found in the views held by the docetic school of the Mahāsunnatāvādins[25] in the age of Asoka who held that the Sangha could not accept gifts or purify them or enjoy, eat and drink, or that gift given to it brought great reward. Here indeed we have an explanation of the curious wording of the donation referred to above. The formal dedication is made to the Cātuddissa Bhikkhu-Sangha, but the pecuniary endowment is made on the real Sangha which is capable of accepting and enjoying gifts.

The Buddhist Sangha existed then originally as a sect of the Paribrajaka community of the 6th century,. B.C. It rested on the basis of a common Dhamma and had at first no special Vinaya of its own. It is impossible to say at what point of time, but certainly very early in its history, the sect of Buddha, the Cātuddisa Bhikkhu-Sangha, devised an external bond of union which was called Pātimokkha. This Pātimokkha seems to have been something quite different in form and significance from what the tem imports to us now. In the Mahāpadāna Sutta, the idea occurs to Vipassi, while staying at Bandhumati, of asking the Bhikkhus living there to go abroad on preaching mission and come back to Bandhumati after every six years in order to recite the Pātimokkha. The Pātimokkha rehearsed by Vipassi is curiously enough something totally different from the Pātimokkha we know of. It consists only of a few hymnal verses which we find incorporated in the Dhammapada. The following are the verses that constitute the Pātimokkha[26]:—

Khanti paramam tapo titikkhā
Nibbānam paramam vadanti Buddhā
Na hi pabbajito parupaghāti
Samano hoti param vihethayanto.
Sabba-pāpassa akaranam, kusalassa upasampadā
Sacitta-pariyodapanam, etam Buddhāna sāsanam.

These verses ending with, etam Buddhāna sāsanam,' are, it will be observed, nothing more than a confession of faith and this confession of faith constituted the Pātimokkha of Vipassi and his followers at Bandhumati. What was then the original connotation and significance of the term, Pātimokkha? What was the original idea of the Buddhist community which it sought to represent? Some light might be thrown on these questions by the etymology of the word, if only we could definitely settle it. "The etymological meaning of a word," says Max Müller, "is always extremely important both psychologically and historically because it indicates the point form which certain ideas started."[27] From this point of view the etymology of the word, Pātimokkha, may be carefully considered, as it might indicate to us the starting point of the later development of the institution of Pātimokkha among the Buddhists.

But here unfortunately we are on slippery ground. Various etymologies have been suggested for the word, Pātimokkha.[28] But in these conjectural etymologies sufficient attention has not been paid to the fact that "the word is older than the present shape of the formulary, now so called."[29] It is futile to foist on a word an etymology which suits only its later developed meaning. Its true etymology however has been indicated by Kern, although his own derivation is fantastic to a degree.

He takes Pātimokkha in the sense of cuirass or something serving as a (spiritual) cuirass and cites as his authority a certain phrase in Anguttara Nikāya and its tīkā.[30] In the original passage in the Anguttara however the phrase, *pātimokkha-samvara-samvuta,* on which Kern relies is a descriptive phrase applying to a good Bhikkhu and can be interpreted only as 'controlled by the restraints imposẹd by the Pātimokkha.' There is absolutely no suggestion of any metaphorical or secondary meaning or pan in the world Pātimokkha, and no such suggestion in the other descriptive phrases occurring in the passage in question.[31] Then the comment of Subhuti taken from an old tīkā suggests nothing.[32] The old commentator was only trying to bring out some hidden significance from the etymology of the word and his ignorance of etymology and grammar can afford us more of amusement than of instruction. But there is really nothing in the tīkā to suggest a cuirass. There is however a cognate word in Pali, *viz.*, Pātimokkho,[33] which means something that is bound on or fixed and hence accoutrement (*c.f.*, Sans. प्रतिमुक्त=परिहितवस्त्रादिरित्यमरः) with which Kern evidently identifies the word; but it is only a cognate and not a synonymous word. Pātimokkha has been equated to Sans. प्रातिमोक्ष which from its etymological parts may be easily and naturally interpreted as something serving as a bond, the prefix प्रति meaning "against" and the root मोक्ष meaning "scattering" (क्षेपणे इति कविकल्पद्रुम), though I have not been able to discover any instance of the use of the word precisely in this sense in Sanskrit. It seems to me that the right etymological interpretation of the word, Pātimokkha, is 'Bond', and it is presumably in this sense that the word is used in the passage in the Mahāpadana Sutta referred to above. The Buddhist Sangha had rested originally on a community of faith and belief, but an external bond of union, a Pātimokkha, was afterwards devised which served to convert this *Sect* into a religious *Order*, and this Pātimokkha originally consisted in periodical meetings for the purpose of holding a communal confession of faith made by means of hymn-singing. This custom is clearly indicated by the story of Vipassi.

The work of the First Council seems to have brought the development of the Pātimokkha a step further. The most important function of the Council was, as I have shown the development of the rules of the Order, a special Vinaya for the Buddhist Sangha, and the form of the Vinaya settled by it was the original form of the Pātimokkha, a bare code of canon law, a mere enumeration and classification of ecclesiastical offences. In the legendary account of the proceedings of the council as given in the 11th khandaka of the Cullavagga, the word, Pātimokkha, is nowhere mentioned, though all the heads of offences are given except the *Sekhiya* and the *Adhikarana Samattha.*[34] The reason for the studied omission of the word Pātimokkha is not far to seek when we consider that at the time when the proceedings were put into the present narrative shape, people understood by Pātimokkha something quite different from a code of Vinaya rules. It may be for the same reason, as Rhys Davids and Oldenberg suggest,[35] that in Bhabrā edict the Pātimokkha is named by Asoka *Vinaya-Samukasa*. The code of Vinaya rules, after the First Council, became the bond of association of the Buddhist Bhikkhus and it came to be called Pātimokkha (Bond).

Now the existence of Pātimokkha originally as a mere code and not a ritual is beyond all legitimate doubt. In the Ākankheyya Sutta, Buddha is represented as enjoining on the Bhikkhus continuance in the practice of Sīla, adhering to the Pātimokkhā (in the plural) and becoming *pātimokkha-samvara-samvuto,* etc.[36] Here the plural, Pātimokkhā, cannot but mean the rules of canon law contained in the code. The phrase, *pātimokkha-samvara-samvuta,* which is of frequent occurrence in the Suttas, has been variously translated, but its obvious meaning is 'controlled by the restraints imposed by the Pātimokkha,' where Pātimokkha is regarded as a code. Besides the most important and convincing piece of evidence that the Pātimokkha was originally in the bare form of a code is the fact that the Sutta-Vibhanga contemplates it as such. In the Sutta-Vibhanga there is not the usual word-for-word commentary on the introductory formular of the Pātimokkha as we now have it. This however is found in the Mahavagga as an incongruous inset.[37] Rhys Davids and Oldenberg regard this inset commentary as belonging to what they call the *Old Commentary of the Pātimokkha.*[38] The learned scholars however put forward no arguments at all in support of this view. I suggest on the other hand that this formular with its commentary was a later invention and the commentary was devised on the lines of the old commentary embedded in the Sutta-Vibhanga only for the sake of completeness.[39] The Sutta-Vibhanga in fact regards the Pātimokkha as a mere *code*, while the Mahavagga regards it as a *liturgy.*

Let us now turn to the contents of the code. The original code appears to have included only 150 rules. Even after it had become a liturgy, the number was the same. In the Samana-vagga of Anguttara, the Vijji-puttaka Bhikkhu says, "Sadhikam idam bhante diyaddhasikkhāpadasatam anvaddhamasam uddesam āgaccheti,[40] referring no doubt to the rules of the Pātimokkha after it had assumed a liturgical form. In the Milindapanho also, we find the number 150. A good Bhikkhu is described as "diyaddhesu sikkhāpadasatesu samādāya vattanto."[41] But in the Pali Pātimokkha that we possess the number of rules is 227. Various suggestions have been made to account for this discrepancy. A comparison of the Pali version of the Pātimokkha with the Chinese and the Thibetan shows differences, both numerical and substantial, in the Pācittiya and the Sekhiya rules, the greater discrepancy being with regard to the latter head.[42] Besides the total number of Sekhiyas is not mentioned as is usual in the Pali version indicating, as some scholars suggest, that they were not strictly a part and parcel of the code, being mere matters of detail, and might be added to or taken away from.[43] But even if we exclude the Sekhiyas, the number comes up to 152 and no calculation can make it exactly 150. The fact probably is that the original code was an elastic one, and before reaching a standard text it underwent various and complicated interpolations which it is now well-nigh impossible for us to detect. A few instances will serve to illustrate this.

It is admitted in the Vinayapitaka[44] that the rehearsal of the Sikkhāpadas was adopted as a congregational liturgy at a later stage in imitation of the rites of the non-Buddhist Paribrajakas. Yet we find Sikkhāpadas in which the liturgical form of the Pātimokkha is clearly recognised (*Pāvittiya*, 72, 73). Then the seven Adhikaranasamatthas seem to stand apart from the rest of the work and have all the appearance of being of later growth. In the First Council there was some dispute as to what were the minor and lesser precepts (khuddānu-khuddakāni sikkhāpadāni). Some said that these referred to all the rules, except the *Pārājikas,* others the *Sanghādiṣesas,* other *Aniyatas*, others *Nissaggiyas*, others *Pācittiyas* and others *Pātidesaniyas.*[45] It will be observed that no one mentioned the *Sekhiyas* and the *Adhikaranasamatthas* and claimed authenticity and primacy for them. Evidently they were considered to be of a somewhat different character from the rest. The Adhikaranasamatthas lay down adjective or procedural law while the rest of the Pātimokkha contains substantive law. Take for instance the case of the 13 rules called *Sanghādisesas*. Certain offences are described in these rules, and the penalties also are prescribed. But nothing is said about the mode of adjudication, though some offences are such as cannot be dealt with without formal and elaborate trial (*e.g.*, Sanghādisesa, 8, which would amount to an Āpattadhikarana and in which the complaint must be proved to be groundless).[46] The difficulty must have been experienced later on and the need felt for codifying procedural law which is done in the Adhikaranasamatthas. Then again the usual interrogatory part does not fit in with this section, for no substantive offences are mentioned here as in the other sections. The forms of procedure also clearly point to the development of separate congregations, within settled boundaries of residence, exercising definite ecclesiastical jurisdiction over individual members belonging to each. As I shall show in Chapter V, this is a much later stage in the growth of the Buddhist Sangha—much later than the time when the code of Pātimokkha was drawn up.

Some rules of the Pātimokkha (*e.g.*, Pācittiya, 69 and 73) assume the existence of forms of procedure which are nowhere found in the Pātimokkha itself but in Cullavagga, I. In Pāc., 69 occurs the phrase *Akatānudhammena* ('not dealt with according to form'). The Vibhanga says that the form contemplated here is Ukkhepaniyakamma, but the Pātimokkha knows nothing of such a form. In Pāc, 73, we have the expression, *Janca tattham āpattim āpanno tanca jathādhammo kāretabbo* (the offence arising therefrom is to be dealt with according to the proper form), which seems to contemplate a Tajjaniya kamma for stupidity.[47] Such expressions as above point to the intrusion into the Pātimokkha of the later elements of developed Vinaya.

Sometimes a rule is introduced into the Pātimokkha in the form in which the Mahavagga and the Cullavagga are cast, representing as if Buddha himself were laying down the rule to the Bhikkhus assembled. The story-part is indeed cut out, but the form of address is maintained perhaps through inadvertence. In Pācittiya, 71, occurs the expression—*Sikkhamānena Bhikkhave bhikkhunā anjātabbam paripucchitabbam paripanhitabbam, ayam tattha sāmīci*—which reads just like a rule in the Mahavagga. In Nissaggiya Pācittiya, 10 also, the form of address, *Bhikkhave,*[48] occurs in a similar recommendatory rule (*e.g.*, cīvaratthikena *Bhikkhave* bhikkhunā veyyāvaccakaro niddisitabbo, etc.).

Then again the classification of offences does not appear to have been made on any initially recognised principle, but is more or less haphazard and promiscuous suggesting,[49] if not actually later additions and alterations, at least the elasticity of the code which offered opportunities for them. Kindred offences are sometimes grouped together and sometimes scattered in different parts under the same head. There are in fact so many irregularities and discrepancies throughout that it is clear that the original code could not have been characterised by rigidity and self-completeness. Take the *Pācittiya* rules for instance. It will be observed that rules 83-93 (except one) hang together and are designated in the Pali book as Ratnavagga, but rule 85 does not fit into it. There is no reason why rule 82[50] of Pācittiya should be placed under that category while rule 30[51] of Nissagiya Pācittiya under another category. The second seems to be only a special application of the first and in the Thibetan version of the Pātimokkha the second rule is excluded.[52] Rules 67 and 45[53] also of Pācittiya are comprehensive enough to cover rules 27 and 30[54] of the same section. Rhys Davids and Oldenberg have uttered a warning against the attempt to trace in such irregularities in arrangement which may very well be due to want of literary clearness in the compilers, any historical argument.[55] But these irregularities show in the first place the original elasticity of the code, in the second place, they become circumstantial evidence, taken together with other facts, of later manipulations of the code. But the Pātimokkha, curiously enough, outgrew the form of a code and developed into a form of confessional service.

References

1. See *Sāmannaphala Sutta* (Digha Nikaya), 2-7. The names are—Purāno Kassapo, Mokkhali-Gosalo, Ajito Kesā-Kambalī, Pakudho Kaccāyano, Sanjayo Belatthiputto, Nigantho Nātha-putto. They are all described as Sanghī Ganī

Ganācariyo, and brief accounts are given of the doctrines held by them. The names occur in many places besides, *e.g.*, Mahāparinibbāna Suttanta. V. 26; Cullavagga V. 8, I; etc.

2. Thus in the sequel to the story of Sanjaya, Maha., 1, 23, Sariputta and Moggallana and with them probably the whole body of Sanjaya's followers receive the *Ehi Bhikkhu Upasampadā* from Buddha (*ibid.*, I. 24.4, 5).

3. See Rhys David's *Buddhist India*, p. 145: "In a note on Panini, IV, 3, 110, there are mentioned two Brahmin Orders, the Karmandinas and the Parasarinas. Now in the Majjhima (3. 298), the opinions of a certain Parasariva, a Brahmin teacher, are discussed by Buddha. It is very probable that he was either the founder or an adherent of the second of these schools. In any case the Order still existed at the time when the note to Panini was made, and it is probably referred to in an inscription mentioned by Cunningham (Arch. R. XX. 105)."

4. *E.g.*, Sanjaye paribbājake, brahmacariyam caranti—Maha, 1.23.1. "Thus in the standing phrase used to state that so and so has become an Arhat, it is said he has realised the aim of the higher life (*Brahmacariya-Pariyosanam*)"—Rhys Davids's *Dialogues of Buddha,* Vol. II, p.192. Oldenberg seems to have noticed this curious resemblance. He says: "The order of Buddhists presents, as long as the master is alive, a union of teachers and scholars after the Brahmanical model." (*Buddha,* translated by Hoey, 1882).

5. The *Oxford New English Dictionary explains* a Sect as a religious following; adherence to a particular teacher or faith. (4th meaning).

6. This word is explained in the *Oxford New English Dictionary* as signifying 'a body or society of persons living by common consent under the same religious, moral or social regulation or discipline; a monastic society or fraternity.' (7th meaning).

7. They are enumerated in the Mahāparinibbāna Suttanta as—Satipatthana, Sammappadhana, Iddhipada, Indriya, Bala, Bhojjhanga, Ariyo Atthangiko Maggo. Rhys Davids has given an analysis of them in *Dialogues of Buddha,* Vol. III, pp. 129-130. See also Hardy's *Netti-Pakarana* (P.T.S.)—Intro., pp. xxx-xxxii.

8. See Ch. IV of the *Rule of St. Benedict,* translated by Gasquet in the King's Classics Series, Chatto and Windus.

9. See Ch. II, 24, 25 (*Digha Nikaya,* P.T.S., Vol. II, pp. 99-100).

10. See Chapter VI of the present thesis.

11. Rhys Davids, *Dialogues of Buddha,* Vol. III, p. 77

12. VI, 1 (D.N., p. 154).

13. See vv. 10-22.

14. धर्म्मस्य शब्दभूलत्वादशक्यमनपेक्ष्य स्यात् । अपित्र कर्त्तृसामान्यात् प्रमाणमनुमानं स्यात् । विरोधेत्वनपेक्षा स्यादसति ह्यनुमान हेतुदर्शनाच्च ।

—Jaimini's Purva-Mimansa, 1, 3, 1-4.

15. *Mahaparinibbana Suttanta,* VI, 20 *e.g.*, Uppadutā ca homa 'Idam vo appati,' etc., idāni pana mayam yam icchissāma tam karissāma, yam na icchissāma tam na karissāmāti.

16. Cullavagga, XI, 1, 16. (V.P., II, p. 292).

17. Oldenberg's *Vinayapitakam,* Vol. I, Intro., pp. xxvi-xxvviii.

18. Mahavagga, VIII, 27.5; Cullavagga, VI, 1.4; *Ibid,* VI, 9,1. *Kutadanta Sutta,* 24 (D.N., Vol. I, p. 145), etc., etc.

19. Inscription at Dambulla Temple in Ceylon (Asoka's time)—*Ind. Ant.*, 1872, p. 139.

    Karle Cave Inscriptions—Ep. Ind., VII, No. 7, pp. 58, 88.

    Nasik Cave Inscriptions—Ep. Ind., VIII, No. 8, pp. 62, 75, 76, 82, 90, etc.

    Mathura Lion-Capital Inscription—Ep. Ind., IX, No. 17 (Circa 120 B.C.)

20. *E.g. Kutadanta Sutta,* 24 (D.N., Vol. I, p. 145)—Cullavagga, VI, 1, 4; *Ibid.*, VI, 9,1.

21. See *Epigraphia Indica,* Vol. VII, pp. 59-60.

22. See Chapter V of this thesis.

23. See Ep. Ind., Vol. VIII, No. 8, p. 90.

24. See *Cetokhila Sutta* (Majjhim Nikaya)—3-6; 15-18. (Translated by Rhys Davids in *Buddhist Suttas,* S.B.E., XI, pp. 224, 228-229).

25. See *Kathavatthu,* Bk. XVII, 6, 7, 8, 9, (Aung and Davids's *Points of Controversy,* P.T.S., 1915, pp. 318-320).

26. See *Mahāpadana Sutta* (Digha Nikaya), 3.28. (D.N., Vol. II, p. 49); *Dhammapada,* 184-6. The last two lines of the verses quoted are not in the *Dhammapada.*

27. Max Müller's *Origin of Religion,* p. 10.

28. *E.g.*

    (*i*) Patimokkhan ti adim etam mukham etam pamukham etam kusalanam dhammanam, tena vuccati patimokkhan ti—Mahavagga, II, 3,4.

    (*ii*) Yo taṃ pati rakkhati tam mokkhati moceti apayikadidukkhehi tasma patimokkhan ti vuccati (an old gloss quoted by Subhuti)—See Childer's *Pali Dictionary,* p. 363.

    (*iii*) Patimokkhan ti etimokkham patippamokkham atisettham atiuttamam—Gloss from *Samantapasādika* quoted by Spiegel (See *Ibid.* p. 363).

    (*iv*) Patimokkha, Disburdening, getting free: Davids and Oldenberg. (*Vinaya Texts,* S.B.E., Pt. I, Intro. xxviii).

    (*v*) Pratimoksa-Cuirass, something serving as a spiritual cuirass: Kern (see *Man. of Ind. Buddhism,* p. 74, footnote 5).

29. See Vinaya Texts, Pt. 1, S.B.E., Intro. p. xxviii.

30. See Kern's *Man. of Ind. Buddhism,* p. 74, footnote 5.

31. *Anguttara,* II, 4, 5. (P.T.S., Pt. 1, p. 63) Idhāvuso bhikkhu sīlavā hoti pātimokkha-samvara-sambhuto viharati ācara-gocara-sampanna anumathesu vijjesu bhaddaassāiva samādāya sikkhati sikkhāpadesu.

32. See *supra,* Footnote, 28 (ii).

33. See Childern's *Dictionary of the Pali Language, ad loc.*

34. See Cullavagga, XI, 1, 9.

35. *Vinaya Texts,* Pt. I, S.B.E., Intro., p. xxvi.

36. See *Akankheyya Sutta,* (translated in *Buddhist Suttas,* S.B.E., see p. 210).

37. See Mahavagga, II, 3, 4-8.

38. See *Vinaya Texts,* Pt. I, S.B.E., Intro. pp. xv-xvi.

39. It will be observed that in the inset commentary (Mahavagga, II, 3.5) in the note on the phrase, 'yassa siya apatti,' offences are divided into two groups—the group of five and the group of seven. This grouping is found in Cullavagga, IX, 3.3, but not in the Pātimokkha itself. Neither of these two groups coincides with the original classification of offences in the Pātimokkha. Some of the offences included in either of the two groups are unknown to it, *e.g., Dukkata, Thullaccaya, Dubbhasita,* while others found in it are omitted, *e.g., Aniyata, Nissaggiya, Pacittiya and Sekhiya.* This re-arrangement of the Pātimokkha classification of offences seems to have been made much later when the whole Vinaya was developed and its adoption in the inset commentary seems to me to point to the later formation of this portion of the commentary.

40. See *Samana-vagga,* III, 83.1 (Anguttara Nikaya, P.T.S., Pt. I, p. 230).

41. See Tenckner's *Milindapanho,* p. 243. The number 150 occurs also at p. 272, *ibid.*

42. See पातिमोक्ष by Bidhusekhar Sastri, pp. 4-5 of *Nivedana.*

43. See *ibid,* p. 233.

44. See Mahavagga, II, 1.

45. See Cullavagga, XI, 1.9.

46. Jo pana bhikkhu bhikkhum dutto doso appatīto amulakena pārājikena dhammena anuddhamseyya appevanāma nam imamhā brahmacariyā cābeyyanti tato aparena samayena samanuggāhiyamāno vā amulakam ceva tam adhikaranam hoti bhikkhus ca dosam patittāti samghādiseso. This would be an *Āpattādhikarana;* See Cullavagga, IV, 14, 10.

47. See Cullavagga, I, 4.1 (*Tajjaniya-kamma* is for a 'bāla' among others).

48. Rhys Davids and Oldenberg say: "This word of address is most noteworthy as standing quite isolated in the Pātimokkha. It must be meant as an address by the Buddha himself to the Brethren; for, if it were the address of the Bhikkhu reciting the Pātimokkha, the expression used would necessarily be 'ayasmanto,' as in the closing words of each chapter, or words to that effect". The learned translators go on to say: "That it should have been left in is a striking proof of the faithfulness with which the Pātimokkha has been preserved. Is it a survival of some form of word older even than the

Pātimokkha? Or is it merely an ancient blunder?" (*Vinaya Texts,* S.B.E., Pt. I, p. 23, footnote). If by faithfulness, the learned translators mean the faithfulness of Ceylonese scribes, I have nothing to say. In the Thibetan *So-sar-thar-pa,* the form of address which was probably felt to be anomalous is deleted. (See J. and P.A.S.B., Vol. XI, Nos. 3 and 4, March and April, 1915—pp. 47-48 and p. 59, *Pāc,* 75, which corresponds to Pali. *Pāc.* 71.) But my point is that the standard text of the Pātimokkha code did not come into existence at once self-complete. Before reaching a standard text, the rules were surely not regarded with any exclusive sanctity, and there were many additions and alterations at different stages. I do not understand the questions raised by the translators. The form of address, anomalously maintained, seems to me to point to later interpolations.

49. Rhys Davids and Oldenberg say:—"Inside each class (off offences), the sequence of the clauses follows no invariable rule. Sometimes offences of a related character are place together in groups, but sometimes those which would naturally come together are found scattered in quite different parts of the same class. It is perhaps worthy of notice that there sometimes seems, as in the two cases first mentioned in the last note, to be an effort to arrange the offences in groups (Vagga) of ten: and in three cases we find regulations formulated with the utmost brevity (the offences being merely expressed by a locative case dependent on *Pācittiyam*) at the commencement of such a vagga."—*Vinaya Texts,* Pt. I (S.B.E., Vol. XIII), Intro. p. xiv.
50. Jo Pana bhikkhu jānam sanghikam lābham parinatam puggalassa parinameyya pācittiyam.
51. Jo pana bhikkhu jānam sanghikam lābham parinatam attano parināmeyya nissaggiyam pācittiyam.
52. See *So-sor-thar-pa* (J.A.S.B., Vol. XI, Nos. 3 and 4, March and April, 1915), edited by S.C. Vidyabhusan, p. 32.
53. Jo pana bhikkhu mātugāmena saddhim sambidhāya ekaddhā namaggam patipajjeyya antamaso gamantarampi pācittiyam *Pāc.* 67: Jo pana bhikkhu mātugāmena saddhim eko ekaya raho nisajjam kappeyya Pacittiyam, *Pāc.* 45.
54. Je pana bhikkhu bhikkhuniya saddhim sambidhaya eka ddhanameggam patipajjeyya antamaso gamantarampi anntra samaya pacittiyam—*Pac.* 27; Jo pana bhikkhu bhikkhuniya saddhim eko ekaya raho nisajjam kappeyya pacittiyam *Pac.* 30.
55. "The irregularities in arrangement may very well be due to want of literary clearness in the compilers of the present Form of Confession, and it would be hazardous to trace in it any historical argument". *Vinaya Texts,* Pt. I (S.B.E., Vol. XIII), Intro., p. xiv.

4

The Pātimokkha as a Ritual

In the previous chapter we have observed that the Buddhist Sangha originated as a mere sect of the Paribrajaka community of the 6th century B.C. Its unity lay in adherence to a common Dhamma, but it had originally no special external bond of union. The Vinaya which it recognised was not a special Buddhist Vinaya. This latter kind of Vinaya in its earliest form was probably settled at the First Buddhist Council which is called the Vinayasangiti in the 11th khandaka of the Cullavagga. It has also been shown that the earliest form of the Vinaya was the code of Pātimokkha. The codified body of rules which was intended specially for the Buddhist Sangha was advisedly called by this name (Pātimokkha—Bond) because it supplied for the Buddhist Bhikkhus an external bond of union. The present ritual form of the Pātimokkha was not its original form—the original was a mere code. It was only subsequently that it became the ground of a Buddhist ritual and was re-edited for that purpose. The *Introductory Formular* at the beginning and the *Interrogatory Portions* appended to each section were obviously later additions.

The Buddhist rite of Uposatha, of which the recital of the Pātimokkha forms the essential part, is at least as old as the Vinayapitaka. But it is certainly not as old as the foundation of the Buddhist Sangha itself. An earlier communal rite is referred to in the story of Vipassi in the Mahāpadāna Sutta, and the later introduction of the Uposatha is also clearly admitted in Mahavagga, II, 1. But the Uposatha ceremony was by no means a Buddhist innovation, for its germs may be traced in a well known Vedic institution, which strikingly exemplifies the dictum of Edward Clodd, stated as it is in an extreme form, that "in religious there are no inventions, only survivals."[1]

The rudimentary idea in the Buddhist Uposatha service seems to be the observance of sacred days. Round about this, certain peculiarly Buddhist ideas have gathered together, *e.g.*, the Buddhist Doctrine of Confession. But the rite itself which is, as I shall show a curious combination of certain distinct ideas, has passed through two principal stages. At first it was of a practical character, being one of the main regulations of monastic life, perhaps the chief instrument of communal self-government in the Buddhist Sangha. But this practical character and purpose of the Uposatha service afterwards evaporated. It became a mere ceremonial observance, serving the same purpose among the Buddhist Bhikkhus as the Holy Communion amongst the Christians, being nothing but the formal embodiment of the corporate life of a cenobitical society resident at an avāsa.

The observance of the sacred days is found in the Vedic times in close and inseparable connection with certain Vedic sacrifices. The days of the Full Moon and the New Moon were from the earliest times in India regarded as sacred for sacrificial purposes. The Full Moon and the New Moon are effusively greeted in two hymns of the Atharaveda.[2] The Vedic sacrifices of Paurnamāsa and Darsa used to be offered on these days. As preliminary to these sacrifices the preceding days had to be kept holy by the intending sacrificer by fasting or partial abstention from food, as well as by retirement at night into the house in which the sacrificial fire was kept.[3] There is a legend in the Satapatha Brāhmana, by no means peculiar or original, that on these days the gods come to dwell with the intending sacrificer.[4] Hence these days, on which the Vrata ceremonies of fasting, etc., were observed were called Upavasatha days ('upa' near and 'vas' to dwell).[5] Tylor has pointed out the world-wide belief existing at all stages of civilization in the close connection between fasting and intercourse with gods.[6] So the Puritan poet of England speaks of "Spare Fast that with the gods doth diet," spiritualising perhaps what was an essentially material conception.[7] Since primitive times the belief in ceremonial observances on these sacred Vrata days must have been one of the basic elements of Indian culture. One is tempted to think that this primitive belief embodied itself in a settled institution first among the adherents of Brahmanical culture and then the institution spread among all classes, even those who never fully abode by the Aryan cult of ritualism and sacrifice. This is suggested by the fact that ceremonial observances on the Vrata days are very intimately connected with the Vedic sacrifices, but among those who are no ritualists and sacrificers, the Jainas for instance, the custom prevails with equal persistence. It is curious to observe how close the resemblance is between the Vrata ceremonies of the Vedic ritualist and the Posadha ceremonies of the Jaina, though the reason for such observances, as stated in the Satapatha-Brāhmana[8] would not apply in the case of the latter. The Jaina retires on these sacred days into the *Posadhasālā* just as the sacrificer would go into the *Agnyāgāra,* and he takes upon himself the vow of the four abstinences (upavāsa), *viz.*, from food (Āhāra), from luxuries (Sarīra-satkāra), from sexual intercourse (Abrahma) and daily work (Vyāpāra).[8a] Similar abstinences are prescribed also for Buddhist laymen who celebrate the occasion by the observance of the Eight Sīlas. But among the religious mendicants the custom seems to have been different from what prevailed among the laity. Another form of sacred-day observance is related of them in Mahavagga, II. 1. The reason for this difference is not far to seek. The 'abstinences' were already implied in the assumption of a life of religious mendicancy and some substitute had to be found among them for these ceremonical abstinences which prevailed among the laity. Such substitute probably was found in religious discourses.

In the Āruneyopanishad, the rehearsal of the Āranyaka and Upanishad 'among all the Vedas' is enjoined on the Sannyasin.[9] It is also said in Mahavagga, II. 1, that the non-Buddhist Paribrajakas would meet together and hold religious discourses on the sacred days of the month—annatitthiyā paribbājakā cātuddase pannarase atthamiyā ca pakkhassa sannipatitvā dhammam bhāsanti. This points to a custom among the

Paribrajakas of observing the sacred days, though not in the manner of lay people, yet in their own characteristic fashion. On these days the Brahmanical Sannyasis would discourse on the Āranyaka and the Upanishad, while the other classes of Paribrajakas would expound their own canonical literature, transmitted by their teachers most probably by word of mouth. In this way religious discourses among the Paribrajakas took the place of the Vrata ceremonies among the sacrificers. But it seems that the custom was but loosely followed among them, as the free, wandering, unsocial life of the Paribrajakas would not tend to the rigid establishment of any custom, and that is perhaps the reason why it is not mentioned more frequently as a rule of Paribrajaka life. The Buddhist Bhikkhus at any rate did not originally follow the custom of ceremonically observing the sacred days by religious discourses.[10] In the Mahāpadāna Sutta, the Bhikkhus meet together once in six years to recite a hymn which constitutes their Uposatha service.[11] But the Bhikkhus afterwards adopted the custom from other sects of Paribrajakas,[12] and its later introduction into Buddhism is further evidenced by the fact that we hear of "ignorant, unlearned Bhikkhus who neither know Uposatha nor the recital of Pātimokkha."[13]

But though the custom of observing the Uposatha days was a common one from the most primitive times, the form which it assumed among the Buddhist Bhikkhus seems to have been peculiar to them. The Mahavagga story tells us that the non-Buddhist Paribrajakas would meet together and merely discourse on their dhamma (sannipatitvā dhammam bhāsanti). The Buddhists were at first enjoined to observe the Uposatha in this very manner[14] and the form of confessional service was developed subsequently. The frame of the Pātimokkha, as it now stands, unmistakably shows that it was intended that during its recitation a guilty Bhikkhu should confess his offence if he had not done so before. The preliminary Nidāna and the interrogatory portion after each section of the code carry this significance, and the addition of these parts to the parts to the code has completely changed, almost beyond recognition, the original character of the Pātimokkha. It is necessary to enquire into this doctrine of Confession which came to be incorporated with the code, transforming its character and investing it with a new purpose altogether.

Now the doctrine of Confession has two branches—a religious and a legal one, the first leading to absolution and the second to the assumption of penal proceedings. The religious confession called *Exomologesis* was an old institution of Christianity. In Buddhism also it is well recognised. In the Pātimokkha four offences of a light nature, called Pātimokkha four offences of a light nature, called Pātidesaniyas, are described and a form of confession is prescribed on following which the guilty person obtains absolution from them. The scope of the doctrine of absolution on confession seems to have been afterwards widened and in Cullavagga, IV.14, 30-31, any light offence (lahuka āpatti) is said to be set at rest on confession by the guilty Bhikkhu. The principle is clearly recognised in Cullavagga, V. 20. 5, where it is said, "Ariyassa vinaye yo accayam accayato disvā yathādhammam patikaroti āyatim samvaram āpajjatīti," as well as in the Nidāna of the Pātimokkha: "āpatti āvikātabbā āvikatā hi' ss phāsu hoti."[15] But there were graver offences for which confession would be no atonement at all. It is difficult to ascertain how these offences would be dealt with before Buddhist monachism had attained to that stage when each Bhikkhu was regarded as the member of a particular Sangha, subject to its disciplinary jurisdiction.[16] This was, as I shall show in the next chapter, a later stage of development and the procedure codified in the section on the Adhikarana-samatthas could not possibly be taken when eremitical habits prevailed among the Bhikkhus. The original codal form of the Pātimokkha belonged to the earlier stage and it is significant that only one group of offences, *viz.*, the Sanghādisesa, is mentioned as coming within the disciplinary jurisdiction of the Sangha and it is in the case of this group only that certain penalties to be imposed upon the Bhikkhu even against his will (mark the word, *Akāmā*, in "tāvatiham tena bhikkhunā akāmā parivatthabbam," etc.), *viz.*, Parivāsa and Mānatta, are laid down. In the case of the other offences, it is nowhere stated or suggested in the Pātimokkha itself that the Sangha should have jurisdiction over them and no mode of exercising such jurisdiction is defined as in the case of the Sanghādisesas. In the following chapters, I shall trace in broad outline how settled cenobitical societies were evolved out of the original eremitical ideal with which Buddhism had started and how these societies or Sanghas came later on to exercise jurisdiction over each individual member. From one group of offences, the Sangha extended its jurisdiction over all the others, and not only the Sanghādisesas but all offences were brought within the range of its disciplinary proceedings. Alongside of it, the procedural law of the Adhikaranasamatthas was gradually developed, and it was at this stage when the jurisdiction of the Sangha was extended over all offences that the idea of *legal* confession was evolved. It led to the adoption by the Sangha of disciplinary proceedings with regard to the guilty member as apart from mere religious confession which led to absolution from the guilt confessed. Confession was the necessary pre-condition of almost all disciplinary proceedings;[17] and on failure to confess (āpattiyā adassane) the guilty member would be punished with suspension from the Sangha (*Ukkhepaniya Kamma*).[18] The incorporation of the doctrine of legal confession with the code was a real necessity as without it the whole code would be mere dead letter and no disciplinary proceedings could be taken upon it. Hence emphasis was laid on the duty of confession, which was indeed the centre point of monastic discipline, and an adventitious solemnity was given to it by prescribing the performance of this duty on the ceremonically sacred days. We are thus in a position to understand not only how the Uposatha became a confessional service, but also why it seems to be peculiar to the Buddhists. It was the distinct outgrowth of Buddhist monastic life. Among those who followed the eremitical ideal of an unsocial wandering life, such a form of religious service would have little utility or significance. But curiously enough this practical character of the confessional service afterwards evaporated and the original idea of a mere ceremonical observance re-asserted itself.

It has been already remarked that "the whole form of the Pātimokkha shows that it was at first intended that a guilty

Bhikkhu should confess his offence during the recitation if he had not done so before."[19] But in Cullavagga IX. 2,1, the Pātimokkha is interdicted for one who has been guilty of any offence; the violation of this interdiction amounting to a *Dukkata*. In Cullavagga, IX. 1,1, Buddha refuses to recite the Pātimokkha because the assembly is not pure. This interdiction is implied in the custom of Parisuddhi before the Uposatha which is elaborated with several illustrations in Mahavagga, II. 27. This was the very negation of the practical character of the Uposatha and the admission of its purely ceremonical character. From being an instrument of monastic discipline, it came to be nothing more than the organised expression of the communal life of the Buddhist community. The unity of the resident monks at an āvāsa was expressed in the common observance of the Uposatha service which could not be validly performed with an incomplete fraternity.[20] The variations which were made on this rule of complete observance were rejected afterwards at the Council of Vesali.[21] If a new community was formed through a schism, the members of it performed independently three kinds of acts—Uposatha, Pavāranā and Kammavācā.[22] If on the other hand the schismatic parties afterwards coalesced, they celebrated their re-union by holding what was called a Sāmaggi-Uposatha.[23] Thus the Uposatha became, though never in form yet in essence, only the outward expression of the religious fellowship of a community of Bhikkhus resident at an āvāsa. It thus ultimately became among the Buddhists a ceremony closely resembling the Holy Communion of the Christians minus of course those rites in the nature of a mysterium which have grown into the latter from a range of primitive ideas with which Buddhism owns no contact. It is interesting to observe that even the Buddhist idea of Parisuddhi before the Uposatha service is paralleled by a similar idea in early Christianity. Certain offences were held to exclude the guilty person from sharing in the Eucharist: these were three groups classified as (*i*) idolatry (including apostacy), (*ii*) adultery and (*iii*) murder.[24] There is this difference however that the exclusion in Christianity was not revocable as in Buddhism. Even in the modern service of the

Holy Communion, the following provision is observed:[25] "If any one of those (intending partakers of the Holy Communion) be an open and notorious evil liver, or have done any wrong to his neighbours, by word or deed, so that the congregation be thereby offended; the curate, having knowledge thereof, shall call him and advertise him, that in any wise he presume not to come to the Lord's Table, until he hath openly declared himself to have truly repented, and amended his former naughty life, that the congregation may thereby be satisfied, which before was offended; and that he hath recompensed the parties, to whom he hath done wrong; or at least declared himself to be in full purpose so to do, as soon as he conveniently may."

References

1. See *The Story of the Primitive Man*, p. 185.
2. A.V. VII, 79, 80.
3. See *Satapatha-brāhmana,* 1.1. 1.8 (fasting), 9 (partial fasting), 11 (retirement at night into the fire-room).
4. *Satapatha-brāhmana,* 1.1. 1.7.
5. *Ibid.*
6. Tylor's *Primitive Culture* (1891), Vol. II, Ch. XVIII, pp. 410 ff.
7. Milton: *"Il Penseroso,* 1, 46.
8. *Vide* 1.1.1.8.11. (The intending sacrificer ought to fast because the gods are not yet feasted and he should lie in the fire-House to keep the gods, who come to dwell, in company.)

8a. See Hoernle's *Uvāsagadasāo* (Bibliotheca Indica), note 87.

9. सर्ब्बेषु वेदेष्वारण्यकमावर्त्तयेदुपनिषदमावर्त्तयेत्—
10. See quotation, *Supra.*
11. See Chapter III.
12. Anujānāmi bhikkhave cātuddase pannarase atthamiyā ca pakkhassa sannipatitun ti—Maha., II, 1.4.
13. Mahavagga, II—17; 21. 2, 3, 4.
14. Anujānāmi bhikkhave cātuddase pannacase atthamivā pakkhassa sannipatitvā dhammam bhāsitun ti—Maha., II, 2.1.
15. See Mahavagga, II. 3.3.
16. See Chapter V of the present thesis.

17. Na bhikkhave apatinnāya bhikkūnam kammam kātabbam (Here follows the enumeration of the different forms of discipline) Yo karevya āpatti dukkatassa—Cullavagga, IV, 7.

18. Cullavagga, I, 25, 1 (*āpattiyā adassane ukkhepaniya-kamma*).

19. *Per* Rhys Davids and Oldenberg—See *Vinaya Texts* (S.B.E.), Pt. III, p. 306, footnote. ·

20. *Cf*, the distinction between *Vagga Uposatha* and *Samagga Uposatha*—Maha, II, 14.2. Read this with II, 2.4. where the Uposatha cannot be held in the absence of a single Bhikkhu—unless (*i*) he has declared his Parisuddi or (*ii*) he has been taken outside the boundary of the āvāsa. It is laid down, "na tv va vaggena sanghena uposatha kātabbo". (See *Digha Nikaya,* P.T.S., Vol. I. p. 122).

21. *Cf*. *Āvāsakappa* (Culla., XII, 2.8)—which is interdicted in Maha., II, 83.

22. Cullavagga, VII, 5.2.

23. *Maha*., II, 36. 4 and X, 5. 14.

24. See *Encyclopædia Britannica* on *Confession* (11th Ed.)

25. See *The Communion Service* (from *Book of Common Prayer*), edited by the Right Rev. John William Colenso, D.D., Lord Bishop of Natal (Macmillan and Co., London, 1886), pp. 1-2.

5

The Growth of the Buddhist Cœnobium

Saint Benedict divides, monks into four classes—Cenobites, Anchorites, Sarabites and Gyrovagi.[1] Among the early Paribrajakas of India, though we find the other three classes, no Cenobites are found. The Paribrājakas are mostly of Anchorite *cum* Gyrovagus character. In the Buddhist sect of the Paribrājakas too the cenobitical ideal seems to have been originally unknown. We find it expressly ruled out in a number of passages cited below which belong to an earlier range of Buddhistic ideas. But with the lapse of time and the growth of the Buddhist Sangha, the communal life of the Bhikkhus came to gravitate more and more towards a cœnobium. The contrast between the earlier eremitical and the latter cenobitical ideal struck Milinda and forms the subject of his enquiry in the 41st dilemma propounded to Nāgasena. Milinda asks:—[2]

"Bhante Nāgasena, bhāsitam p'etam Bhagavatā;

Santhavāto bhayam jātam, niketā jāyatī rajo,

Aniketam asanthavam, etam ve munidassanamti

Puna ca bhanitam:

Vihāre kāraye ramme, vāsay' ettha bahussute ti.

* * * *

Ayam pi ubhayokotiko panho

tavānuppatto, so tayā nibbahitabbo ti."

For the solution of such problems, it is only the historical method of enquiry, which a learned English writer has aptly called 'a key to unlock ancient riddles, a solvent of apparent contradictions, a touch-stone of sophistries'[3] that can be really helpful. But of this, of course, neither the simple-minded King nor his eloquent preceptor knew anything whatever. The fact is that the Munisutta[4] from which Milinda quotes belongs to a stage in the evolution of Buddhist communal life which had already passed away when the second gāthā was composed. Between the two intervenes a considerable period of evolution, of modification, development and growth.

In numerous passages of Buddhist canonical literature, settled life in a monastery is not contemplated at all and the ideal life for a Bhikkhu is set out to be a free, unsocial, eremitical one. In Mahavagga, I. 11, we find Buddha insisting on unsocial life in its extreme form—Mā ekena dve agamittha (Let not two of you go the same way), and in Mahāparinibbāna Sutta, I. 6, we find him declaring, "Yāvakīvan ca bhikkhave bhikkhū ārannakesu senāsanesu sāpekhā bhavissanti, vuddhi yeva bhikkhave bhikkhūnam pātikankhā no parihāni" (as long as the Bhikkhus delight in forest-seals, so long they my be expected not to decline, but to prosper). The eremitical ideal indicated here—a life of solitude and hardship—is that set forth in the so-called four Nissayas[5] which constitute a curious formal survival in the Ordination ceremony of modern Buddhism from a stratum of primitive ideas which has long since worn away. In these are recommended to the Buddhist neophyte four ascetic and eremitical practices; *viz.*, *Pindiyālopa bhojanam* (mendicancy), *Pamsukūlacīvaram* (clothing in cast-off rags), *Rukkhamūlasenāsanam* (sitting and lying at the foot of a tree) and *Pūtimuttabhesajjam* (using urine as medicine). Exceptions to these practices are admitted, but not recommended.[6] The same eremitical ideal is insistently harped upon in the Suttanipāta which certainly contains some of the oldest passages of primitive Buddhism.[7] Thus the whole Khaggavisāna Sutta[8] with its refrain, Eko care khaggavisānakappo (Let him wander alone like a rhinoceros), is devoted to the exaltation of it. The same ideal is to be found also in the Sāriputta Sutta[9] in which the Bhikkhu who is loath of the world and affects an isolated seat or the root of a tree or a cemetery or who lives in the caves of the mountains is extolled.[10] In many hymns of the Dhammapada and the Theragāṭhā this praise of eremitical life is repeatedly echoed. The following hymns for instance recommends aloofness from the society not only of house-holders, but also of homeless Bhikkhus:

Asamsattham gahatthehi anāgārehi c'ūbhayam

Anokasārim apiccham tamaham brūmi brāhmanam.[11]

Again the ideal extolled in the following hymn has nothing to differentiate it from the ideal of a Brahmanical ascetic or Sannyāsi:

Pamsukūladharm jantum kisam dhamanisanthatan

Ekamvanasmin jhāyantam tamaham brūmi brāhmanam.[12]

Unsocial life is again emphasised in the following:

Ekassa caritam seyyo n'atthi bāle sahāyitā

Eko care na ca pāpāni kariyā

Appossukko mātang' aranne vā nāgo.[13]

And,

Ekāsanam ekaseyyam ekocaramatandito

Eko damayamattānam vanante ramito siyā.[14]

In the Milindapanho an old gāthā is quoted the antiquity of which is indicated by the curious legend that it was uttered by Brahma Sampati in the presence of the Tathāgata, as also by the fact that it occurs both in the Theragāthā and the Samyutta Nikāya:

Sevetha pantāni senāsanāni

Careyya samyojanavippamokkhā

Sace ratim nādhigacchayya tattha

Samghe vase rakkhitatto satīmā ti.[15]

The shelter of the Sangha, as is said here, is to be sought only by those who find no peace in solitude, the unsocial life is preferred to cenobitical society. The ascetic eremitical practices mentioned above were classified in later literature as the 13 Dhutangas.[16] The practice of them was supposed to bring exceeding great reward and Nāgasena grows ecstatic over them.[17]

This ideal of life, it will be observed, is in perfect keeping with the rules of a wandering mendicant's life as set forth in the Upanishads. The Āruneya says: "वर्षासु ध्रवशीलोइष्टौ मासानेकाकी यतिश्चरेद द्वावेव वा."[18] The Yati or Sannyasi "as a rule is to make his home by the side of water, on sandbanks in a river or before the doors of a temple or to sit or lie on the bare earth. According to Jābāla, 6, he should remain homeless in a deserted house, or a temple of the gods, on a heap of grass, or an antheap or among the roots of a tree, in a potter's shed, by a sacrificial fire, on an island in a river, in a cave in the mountains, a glen, or a hollow tree, by a waterfall or on the bare earth."[19] There can be no doubt that such unsocial, ascetic and eremitical life was originally contemplated by the Buddhists too. Afterwards it remained only as an ideal while the actual practices of the Buddhist Bhikkhus diverged more and more from it. As the āvāsas were staked out, vihāras constructed, and cenobitical societies gradually developed and organised, the ideal of eremitical life was thrust more and more into the back ground. Observe how the Four Nissayas—one of the cardinal parts of primitive Buddhism—were substantially modified later on in practice. Mendicancy was at first the rule. But the piety of lay devotees often alleviated the rigours of mendicant life. We hear of householders' giving *Perpetual alms* to the Sangha[20] or making generous gifts of robes[21] or keeping up at Vesali a regular service of sweet food[22] or a high official at Court, a follower of the Ājīvakas, providing the day's meal for the Sangha.[23] It was indeed suggested by Devadatta that accepting invitations was inconsistent with the principle of mendicancy.[24] When monasteries came into existence, the resident monks would receive endowments from pious Upāsakas,[25] and sometimes Buddhist kings patronised monastic communities by remitting the revenues of a number of villages which was indeed a long established custom when Chinese pilgrims began to come to India. Thus mendicancy became optional, provision being otherwise made for the support of the Bhikkhus. To be an avowed Pamsukūla (sabbapaṃsukūlika), instead of being a point of merit, was held to constitute a Dukkata.[26] The rule about living at the foot of a tree was modified, if not completely negatived, by the habits of monastic life. Medicaments also were liberally allowed and the whole 6th khandaka of the Mahavagga is a treatise on them. Thus the Nissayas, which are still recommended to a Buddhist neophyte, came to be virtually mere matters of taste and option: Devadatta got no credit for enjoining strictness with regard to some of them.[27]

But all these significant changes notwithstanding it seems that the eremitical principle contended with and perhaps dominated over the cenobitical principle for a long time and it may be that the earliest episode of a conflict between the two principles is contained in the story of Devadatta, who appears to have attempted unsuccessfully at a revival of the older ideal. Even after the institution of monasteries, numerous Bhikkhus retained their eremitical habits living in forests, feeding solely on alms, dressing in cast-off rags, and possessing only three pieces of cloth (ārannakā pindapātikā, pamsukūlikā, tecīvarikā).[28] In Cullavagga, VIII, 6, certain rules are laid down expressly for Ārannaka Bhikkhus. The story of Dabbo (Culla, IV. 4, 4) is an illustration in point. Dabbo is appointed chamberlain (senāsanagāhāpaka) of the āvāsa and he is approached by many Bhikkhus asking for seats (senāsana). We should ordinarily expect the Bhikkhus to lodge together at a monastery. But in the story, the Bhikkhus ask for senāsanas at different parts of Rajagaha lying wide apart, which betrays clearly the survival of the old preference for individualistic and eremitical habits of life.

In the all too meagre accounts that have been left to us of the Sramanas by the Macedonians and the Greeks, we come across no reference to monasteries till we reach Bardesanes in the latter half of the second or the beginning of the 3rd century A.D. Bardesanes is reported to have said of the Shamans, that 'they have houses and temples of a royal foundation and in them stewards who receive from the king a certain allowance of food.'[29] The origin of Bardesanes's information may be safely put a few centuries back—for what was known of India by the Hellenistic world in the second century, A.D. was nothing but the echo of an echo. But a reference to monasteries like this is not to be found in earlier literature, mostly composed though it is of cloying legends conveyed from book to book. For instance, Clemens Alexandrinus (200 A.D.) whose account of the Indian Gymnosophists is obviously a citation from Megasthenes's lost work, *Ta Indika,* refers to the Buddhists as 'philosophers who follow the precepts of Boutta and worship a kind of pyramid beneath which they think the bones of some divinity lie buried.'[30] Here the Chaitya is referred to, but no Vihāra. Going back a little earlier, we find Kleitarchos (quoted by Strabo) saying: "The Pramnai (corruption of Sramana) are philosophers opposed to the Brachmanes and are contentious and fond of argument. They ridicule the Brachmanes who study physiology and astronomy as fools and imposters."[31] Some of these are called the Pramnai of the mountains, others the Gymnetai (which might refer to the Acelakas or the Jaina Digambaras or the Munis,[32] nakedness being common to different classes of ascetics and paribrajakas) and others again as the Pramnai of the city or the Pramnai of the country. Kleitarchos must have jumbled together here different sects and conditions of religious wanderers, but he does not allude to any habitation of any of these sects. We look in vain through all the contemporary Greek accounts, 'obscured and blemished with fables,' for a single reference to a monastery such as we find in the report of Bardesanes, though it conveys information to us not at second but fourth hand. The evidence of the Greek accounts however is purely negative and the sum-total of information that can be gathered from them is that for a long time after the Macedonian invasion Buddhist monasteries were neither numerous nor striking enough to attract the notice of foreigners. The view of vihāras taken by Nāgasena in the 2nd century B.C., as his second argument in defence of monasteries,[33] is significant and suggestive. Nāgasena says that the Sangha becomes easily accessible (sulabhadassana) by having a localised centre. His idea evidently was that the Vihāras were serviceable as head-quarters, so to speak, of the Sangha, the real communal life of which lay outside. In the Milindapanho in fact the eremitical ideal is upheld,[34] though monastic life is admitted as a fact. There is little occasion for doubt that the eremitical principle held sway for a long time even after cœnobium had been developed among the Buddhist Bhikkhus.

At first the Vihāras served as mere lodging-places of individual Bhikkhus. They were no monasteries, no Saṅghārāmas, properly so called, but were rather like the *lauras* organised by St. Sabas in the Holy Land 'wherein a semi-eremitical life was followed, the monks living in separate huts within the enclosure.' The vihāras likewise were generally located in the pleasure-grounds (ārāmas) of kings or of wealthy persons which were often marked off by bamboo-fences or thorn-fences or ditches[35] and were kept in order by a superintendent, employed by the donor, called Ārāmika.[36] But some vihāras were also built in the clearings of forests.[37] In these vihāras the Bhikkhus could take refuge from the inclemencies of weather and climate, and that this was their original purpose is indicated by the gāthās in which Buddha thanked the Setthi of Rajagaha who was the first to build lodging-places for the Bhikkhus.[38] The word, Vihāra, 'in late times almost always was used to designate the whole of a building where many Bhikkhus resided; in older literature, the dwelling-place, the private apartments of a single Bhikkhu.'[39] That the first vihāras were of this character, the separate lodging-places of individual Bhikkhus, is borne out by the evidence of archæology. "The oldest Vihāras," says Fergusson,[40] "consist of one cell only; little hermitages in fact for the residence of a single ascetic. In the next class they were extended to a long verandah with one cell behind it, as in the example, Fig. I. As these had however several doors opening outwards, they probably were divided by partitions internally. In the third class, and by far the most numerous class, Fig. II, the cell expands into a hall, generally with pillars in the centre; and around this the cells of the monks are arranged, the abbot or prior generally occupying cells at either end of the verandah." These three types of monasteries represent with curious exactness the modification of the individualistic cremitical life and the corresponding growth of collective cœnobium among the Bhikkhus. The sixty vihāras built by the Setthi of Rajagaha in one day must have been vihāras of the first type.[41] But vihāras of the second type also are frequently referred to in older Pali literature: the entire monastery consisting of the whole ractangular structure being called Vihāra and the separate cells into which it is divided called Parivenas.[42] In older Pali literature, the word, Vihāra, is used promiscuously to signify either the first type or the second. A vihāra may thus mean the cell of a single Bhikkhu (*e.g.*, the vihāra of the Upajjhāya)[43] or an entire dwelling-place with several cells. Thus it is said, that a vihāra might be built for a number of Bhikkhus or for a single Bhikkhu.[44] But the third type of monasteries is not alluded to in early Pali literature, and the Bhikkhus are put to curious shifts for want to it. The inconvenience of the absence of a hall where the whole body of resident monks could be gathered together was very much felt in connection with the Uposatha service. The service used to be held at first in successive cells;[45] then a whole vihāra was set apart for the purpose which was called Uposathaghara (wrongly translated as the 'Uposatha-hall').[46] Yet a large part of the assembly had to sit outside and the limits, within which all the assembled Bhikkhus would be regarded as constituting the Uposatha assembly called Uposatha-pamukha, were artificially devised by landmarks.[47]

The transition from the eremitical to the cenobitical manner of life was brought about by the institution of Vassa. Paribrajakas of all denominations, it seems, used to observe the rain-retreat. The rule for the Brahmanical Paribrajaka simply lays down that he should be ध्रुवशील during the rains.[48] The period is stated in the Āruneya to be four months. The Jainas have more elaborate rules about the observance of the Pajjusan.[49] The period commences when one month and 20 nights of the rainy season have elapsed, but it is allowable to commence the Pajjusan earlier, though not later.[50] The Buddhist Bhikkhus also followed the custom of all paribrajakas and they had two periods for Vassa, the earlier commencing from the day after the full moon of Āsālha and the later a month after that date, the double period being probably of very ancient origin.[51] This custom of observing the rain-retreat was in its origin presumably nothing but an enforced necessity in the tropical rains of northern India when wandering about was a physical impossibility.[52] But it seems to have assumed with lapse of time some sort of ceremonical significance. It is observed by anthropologists that "when the original purpose of a thing is forgotten or mystified or when the use of it is restricted to a class, time and authority combine to invest it with sanctity."[53] The rain-retreat of the Paribrajakas is a very good illustration in point. In its origin it had a practical purpose. Regularly at a certain season of the year the religious wanderer was forced to take up a local habitation. As the habit emerged into self-consciousness, it hardened into a custom. The original purpose came to be lost sight of more and more and the custom gained a corresponding accession of sanctity. It thus came to be formally enjoined as an indispensable observance for a Sannyasi, Yati or Bhikkhu. The details of the custom however as it obtained among the Brahmanical Paribrajakas are obscure, and we are not privileged to know whether they lived during the rain-retreat separately or collectively. But the Jainas and the Buddhists at any rate spent the rain-retreat in collective bodies. In the Mahāparinibbāna Sutta, for instance, Buddha calls upon the Bhikkhus to spend the Vassa "each according to the place where his friends, acquaintances and inmates may live" round about Vesali. (samantā vesālim yathā-mittam yathā-sandittham yathā-sambhattam vassam upetha).[54]

Out of this institution of rain-retreat which must have existed among the Buddhists from the very beginning, the Āvāsas afterwards originated. The āvāsas were originally colonies staked out for the purpose of sojournment by the Bhikkhus during the rain-retreat. It was only during the period of the vassa that the Bhikkhu had right to a Senāsana (seat) at an āvāsa.[55] To these āvāsas flocked from all quarters Buddhist wandering mendicants during the months from the middle of Āsādha or Srāvana to the middle of Kārtika. During these months therefore the Buddhist Paribrajakas were split up into separate bodies residing at different āvāsas, and it was thus that the āvāsa came gradually to be the unit of Buddhist communal life, the residents in an āvāsa constituting together one complete communion. The limits of the communion were definitely circumscribed.

The limits (sīmā) had to be fixed by a formal Resolution (natti) and would generally coincide with natural boundaries such as a mountain, a rock, a wood, a tree, a path, an ant-hill, a river or a piece of water,[56] but they must not extend beyond three yojanas, nor to the opposite side of a river unless there were facilities for crossing.[57] Where no such boundaries could be fixed, the boundaries of the village or of the market-town (gāmasīmā or nigamasīmā) would serve the purpose.[58] In a forest the community of residence would extend to a distance of seven *abbhantaras*. A river, sea or natural lake could not be a boundary. (Observe an inconsistency here.) In a river, sea or natural lake the limits extended as far as an average man could spurt water all around.[59] Two boundaries must not overlap and one must not encompass the other: an interstice must be left between them.[60] An āvāsa was in this way converted into a definitely circumscribed colony of Bhikkhus. Its corporate communal life was expressed in the congregational Uposatha service, in which *all* the residents of the āvāsa were bound to join either by personal attendance or by a proxy to whom the Chanda or consent of the absentee member had been declared.[61] If one could not join in the congregational service, he must for the time being remain outside the boundary.[62] Emphasis is laid on the completeness of the fraternity present at the congregational service the holding of which with an incomplete communion would amount to a Dukkata.[63] If robes were given to a boundary (sīmā), they must be distributed among all Bhikkhus resident within it.[64] There existed however some āvāsas which shared all profits in common (samābalābhā) and when a gift of robes was made to one of them, it was divided among all[65]—a custom which reminds us of the grouping of monasteries into congregations or orders among the Black Monks of the 13th century. But this idea was not fully carried out in Buddhist monachism. At the periodical distribution of robes again common residence in an āvāsa as well as the condition of the Bhikkhu's clothes was laid down as a necessary condition (Palibodha of Kanthina).[66] The āvāsas thus came to be definite congregational organisations, each self-contained within its own boundary. In later times each congregation began to develop a distinct and separate individuality of its own, but in the beginning the āvāsas must have fully shared in the entire, undivided life of the whole Buddhist community.

It was in these primitive āvāsas that early Pali literature had its origin and growth. In Buddhist canonical literature one comes across among legendary materials realistic descriptions of the sort of life lived at an āvāsa. The night is far spent in one āvāsa in earnest, many-sided debate—some Bhikkhus reciting the dhamma, the Suttantikas propounding the suttantas, the Vinayadharas discussing the vinaya and the Dhamma-kathikas conversing about the dhamma.[67] At the time when āvāsas began to develop, the Bhikkhus had already come into a rich heritage of ecclesiastical laws, legal commentaries, hymns, fables and philosophic speculations which provided for them a none too inconsiderable intellectual pabulum. This cloistral learning went on being modified, developed and systematised at the āvāsas by the Suttantikas, the Vinayadharas, the Dhammakathikas and other professors of monastic learning. The Pitakas were not yet closed and there was still ample scope for the play of original thought and speculation. "It is evident," says Rhys Davids,[68] "that at the time when the suttantas were put together as we have them the legendary material current among the community was still in a fluid, unstable condition, so that it was not only possible, it was considered quite the proper thing to add to or to alter it." The origins of the titles, Suttantika, Vinayadhara, Dhammakathika, Agatāgama, Dhammadhara, Mātikādhara, are obscure, but that they indicated different offices and functions and were not mere honorary titles is evidenced by the occurrence of these names in several inscriptions,[69] and there is little room for doubt that among the Bhikkhus there were professors and specialists who were regarded as the repositories of different branches of traditionary lore. Some of the leading features and ideas of early Buddhism may be presumed to have been evolved at the āvāsas at a time when they shared the communal life of the entire Buddhist community in common. The old commentary on the Pātimokkha, the formulation of Buddhist tenets (*e.g.*, sattatimsa bodhapakkiyā dhammā), the development of the idea of the eternity of Buddha's religion by connecting it with Brahmanical mythological materials,[70] the didactic refashioning of current folklore (found often in the Pitakas, without the Jātaka setting, to point a moral only)[71] in the light of the world-wide theory of metempsychosis,[72] the invention of anecdotal stories and reshaping of traditions about Buddha for the purpose of using the authority of his name to support new rules or old practices, which led ultimately to the remoulding of the legendary setting of the whole of Buddhist literature, the hymns of the Theras and the Theris, of *Dhammapada, Udāna,* etc.,—all these were the work of the primitive āvāsas. It should be remembered that the āvāsas, when all these many-sided literary activities were going on in them, had not yet become distinct, self-centred organisations. The Bhikkhus at the time lived a semi-eremitical life, the āvāsas being resorted to as convenient shelters during rain-retreat. For the best part of the year the Bhikkhus wandered about, constantly meeting together at common meeting places and wayside rest-houses[73] where there was free interchange of thoughts and ideas. There were at that time no sectarian divisions rooted to the soil like the Jetavaniyas, Pubbaseliyas, Aparaseliyas, Rājagiriyas, etc. Hence the intellectual and academic work of the āvāsas was the common property of the whole Buddhist community and, when later on sects began to arise among them, this old learning was recognised as the common basis of them all.

The rules laid down in Cullavagga, VI, 11.3-4, about the allotment of senāsanas at an āvāsa throw some light on the later growth of the āvāsas. It is said that the Senāsanas are to be retained only during the period of the Vassa. In accordance with this rule there are two regular occasions for the allotment of seats, *viz.*, the commencement of the earlier and that of the later Vassa. But curiously enough a third, *viz.*, the day after the Pavāranā, called Antarāmuttaka (which is translated as 'that which involves giving up for the intervening period') is recognised when seats are allotted for the next rain-retreat in anticipation. This antarāmuttaka allotment would be quite superfluous if residence at a monastery were really limited to the period of the rain-retreat. The āvāsas from being shelters during the rain-retreat had become places of domicile and hence seats had to be allotted not only for the three or four months of the year, but also for the remaining months. The modification of the wandering habit of the monks necessitiated the second rule. The fiction, however, *viz.*, that the āvāsas were intended only for rain-retreat and nothing more and that the Bhikkhus should be homeless beyond that period is piously kept up. The allotment which is really made for the non-vassa period is said to be made in advance for the next vassa period, which is unintelligible considering that for that period another allotment is provided for.

With the gradual modification of the itinerant and eremitical character of the Buddhist Bhikkhus, the āvāsas came to be more and more distinct from each other, each having a self-contained and separate communal life. The original Cātuddisa Sangha was permanently broken up into many *sanghas* belonging to different āvāsas and marked off from one another. Thus we find the corporate limits of each sangha carefully demarcated by a variety of rules and regulations. Among the 24 disqualifications which would disentitle a Bhikkhu to become the member of a sangha proceeding to perform an ecclesiastical act are two, *viz.*, 'being of another communion' (nānāsamvāsaka) and 'living outside the boundary' (nānāsīmāya thita).[74] The protest of such a Bhikkhu at an ecclesiastical act is ineffectual.[75] On the eve of the rain-retreat no allotment of Senāsana was made for a Bhikkhu residing outside the boundary of the āvāsa (nissīme thitassa).[76]

Among the rules for the proper observance of the Uposatha, it is enjoined that a Bhikkhu on the Uposatha day must not change to an āvāsa (except under certain conditions) where there are Bhikkhus belonging to a different communion from his own (nānāvāsaka)[77] apparently for the reason that the Uposatha must be held with the Samānavāsakas only which follows from Mahavagga, II, 34.10, *et seq.* On a similar principle it is laid down that a Bhikkhu on his Parivāsa should not go away from one āvāsa to another where Bhikkhus are living, but where there might be Bhikkhus of other communities (nānāvāsaka). But the injunction is modified in the case of a change to a residence of Bhikkhus of the same community (samānavāsaka) under certain circumstances (*viz.*, if the journey took no more than a day).[78] The fact implied in such rules that a Bhikkhu, wherever for the time being the might choose to be, was recognised as belonging to that āvāsa where he was bound to spend the rain-retreat (a senāsana would not be provided for him elsewhere) is interesting as throwing light on the process of growth of later Buddhist sects bearing place-names. Each āvāsa became a distinct centre of monastic life and canonical culture. We hear for instance of the Sāvatthiya Sangha (Mahavagga, III, 13.1), the Vesālika Vijjiputtaka Bhikkhus (Cullavagga, XII, 1), etc. These separate Sanghas were in fact the cradles of the later sects bearing place-names. It should be noted here in passing that the limits of an āvāsa did not always or necessarily coincide with the limits of the Sangha. In Mahavagga, X, 1.9, the question is raised as to what would happen if two schismatic factions wanted to hold Uposatha and perform ecclesiastical acts within the same boundary. It is held there that they are at liberty to do so, as they belong to different communions, though living in the same āvāsa. Hence a distinction is sometimes drawn between 'residence within the common boundary' and 'membership of the same communion.' The case discussed in Mahavagga, X, 1.9, became however one of the ten theses (*viz.*, āvāsakappa) at the council of Vesali and it was dismissed in a somewhat cavalier fashion and in tacit contravention of the above text,[79] on the authority of another text, *viz.*, II, 8.3.

The growth of the early pre-Mahāyāna Buddhist sects is a subject that still awaits investigation by a competent scholar. The genesis of these sects will probably be found to break up into a net-work of various causes. The process of their growth was certainly not unilinear. In Chapter V of the Mahāvamsa are enumerated 18 sects, including the orthodox Theravada, which came into existence within two hundred years of Buddha's decease. Of them, the following sects derive their names from the places where they were to be originally found:—

Gokulika, Cetiya, Himavata, Rājagiriya, Pubbaseliya, Aparaseliya, Vajiriya. Some fresh local sect-names occur in the familiar standardised classification, *viz.*,[80] Avantika, Mahāvihāra, Jetavaniya, Abhayagirivāsin.

Some of these sects are of Ceylonese origin, *e.g.*, Cetiya, Abhayagirivāsin; others evidently originated in northern India;[81] others again are difficult to localise. The origin of such sects must needs be traced in the centralisation of communal life at different āvāsas, which were self-contained and self-governing, and developed later on distinct corporate character. We have seen how completely the Buddhists went back on the original eremitical and gyrovagic ideal. It is further attested by the fact that in later times the Bhikkhus came to be differentiated from the Paribrajakas.[82] The Bhikkhus developed a cenobitical way of life which became their distinguishing feature marking them off from the other Paribrajakas who retained their nomadic, itinerant habits.

In the prolific and wide-spread legends of Barlaam and Josaphat there is a curious passage in which the Indian monastic system is declared to be an imitation from Egypt.[83] The story of Barlaam and Josaphat is an Indian story put into shape by some early Christian writer. It is well-known that the out-look on history of the early Christians was narrowly circumscribed by religious prepossessions and prejudices. Every event in the world's history was by them sought to be brought into connection with the central fact of Christianity. Anachronism was no bar to their systematic Christian interpretation of universal history. There is therefore nothing surprising in the fact that the inventor of the myth of the Egyptian origin of Indian monachism gaily ignored the long period of nearly eight hundred years that intervened between its founder and Antony and Pachomius. Such tempting myths however though doomed to death are fated not to die, and we find even Sir William Jones speculating on the Egyptian relations of Indian monasteries. It is nevertheless exceedingly interesting to notice the parallel developments of Egyptian and Indian monachism.[84] In Egypt as in India the institution of monachism was at first of a purely eremitical character. The life led by the earliest Egyptian monks in the deserts of Nitria, Cellia and Scete is known to us from *Historia Monachorum* and the writings of Rufinus and St. Jerome. In Cellia, the cells of the hermits "stood out of sight and out of earshot of one another; only on Saturday and Sunday did the monks assemble for the services; all the other time was spent in complete solitude, no one ever visiting another except in case of sickness or for some spiritual need."[85] Here we have a resemblance to the individualistic habits of the early Buddhist eremites and the earliest form of the Uposatha service such as is described in the Mahāpadāna Sutta where the Bhikkhus having little touch with one another assemble from distant parts to hold the Uposatha together. But Egyptian monachism did not rest in this eremitical ideal. In Mount Nitria there existed a monastic colony closely resembling a Buddhist āvāsa, but here also the eremitical principle was predominant. In the Pachomian institutions the next stage in the development of monastic life in Egypt is reached. Under St. Pachomius the Egyptian monks became a true religious order, living under a Rule analogous to the Pātimokkha code of the Buddhists. In the description of the Pachomian monastery at Banopolis, which has been left to us by Palladius, we observe 'fully constituted and indeed highly organised cenobitical life,'[86] such as existed no doubt in the later stages of the Buddhist āvāsas, each being an organised self-contained and self-governing colony. Thus the natural transition from the eremitical to the cenobitical life among the early Buddhists in India is exactly paralleled by the process of evolution followed by the Christian monachism of Egypt.

References

1. See the *Rule of Saint Benedict,* Ch. 1, translated by Gasquet in the King's Classics Series, Chatto and Windus. The following summary will suffice. The cenobites are those who live in a monastery under a rule or an Abbot. The Anchorites are in effect those who do not belong to any cenobitical society. The Sarabites are unschooled and undisciplined monks who 'lie to

God by their tonsure. The Gyrovagi are those who move about all their lives through various countries, 'who are always on the move and never settle down.' By anchorites, Saint Benedict specially alluded to the Syrian monks who passed from the monastery into eremitical life. Among the Indian Paribrājakas, Sarabites were by no means uncommon. They were those, who according to Nāgasena, "joined the Order in terror at the tyranny of Kings, or through fear of robbers, or harassment of debts or hope of gaining a livelihood."—See Tenckner's *Milindapanho,* p. 32.

2. See Tenckner's *Milindapanho,* p. 211.
3. See Sir Frederick Pollock's *Oxford Lectures and Other Discourses,* p. 42.
4. In *Suttanipāta*.
5. Mahavagga I, 30.4 and 77.
6. These are called *Atirekalābho* (translated as extra allowances).
7. About the primitive character of *Sutta-nipāta,* see Fausböll's Introduction to the Translation of *Sutta-nipāta* in S.B.E., Vol. X, Fausböll says: "The collection of discourses, *Sutta-nipāta** * * * is very remarkable, as there can be no doubt that it contains some remnants of primitive Buddhism. I consider the greater part of the Mahavagga and nearly the whole of Atthakavagga as very old. I have arrived at this conclusion from two reasons, first from the language and secondly from the contents." The learned translator says further, "We see here a picture not of life in monasteries, but of the life of hermits in its first stage."—Intro. p. xii.

   In the preface to the *Sutta-nipāta* (P.T.S.), Fausböll adds the Parāyanavagga to Mahāvagga and Atthakavagga. (See p. IV) The whole subject of the character of *Sutta-nipāta* is discussed by Rhys Davids in *Buddhist India,* pp. 177-79.
8. Included in the Uragavagga.
9. Included in the Atthakavagga which Fausböll considers to be very old—see *supra*.
10. See Fausböll's *Sutta-Nipāta* (P.T.S.), 958:

    Bhikkhuno vijigucchato

    Bhajato rittam asanam

    Rukkhamūlam susanam vā

    Pabbatanam guhāsu vā.
11. See Fausböll's *Dhammapada,* No. 404.
12. *Ibid.*, No. 395.
13. *Ibid.*, No. 330.
14. *Ibid.*, No. 305.
15. See Tenckner's *Milindapanho,* p. 402. See also *The Questions of Milinda,* Pt. II, p. 343, footnote 3.
16. See *Parivāra,* passim, and elsewhere. For a list of Dhutangas, see Kern's *Manual,* pp. 75-76.

17. The whole of the Navamavagga (pp. 348-362) is devoted to an exaltation of them. Notice specially the 28 advantages that are supposed to accure from their observance.
18. See *Āruneyopanishad*, 4.
19. Deussen's *The Philosophy of the Upanishads*, pp. 380-381.
20. Cullavagga, IV, 4.6.
21. Mahavagga, VIII, 32.1; 1.35.
22. Cullavagga, V, 14.1.
23. Cullavagga, VI, 10.1.
24. The suggestion is made in the 2nd. proposal made by Devadatta, *viz.*, yāvajīvam pindapātikā assu, yo nimantanam sādiyeyya vajjam nam phuseyya (Cullavagga, VII, 3.14). The proposal of Devadatta about a stricter rule of mendicancy is in accordance with the eleemosynary rules of the Jainas (see *Acārānga Sutra*, Bk. II, Lecture 1, Lesson, *et. seq.*— in Jacobi's *Jaina Sutras,* S.B.E., Pt. 1, p. 92 ff.)
25. This is attested by numerous donative inscriptions, too numerous to mention in detail here. See for example the Nasik and Karle cave inscriptions in vols. VII and VIII of *Epigraphia Indica.*
26. Cullavagga, V, 10.2.
27. See the story of Devadatta in Cullavagga, VII, 3, *et. seq*.
28. Mahavagga, VII, 1.1; Cullavagga, XII, 1.8; and elsewhere.
29. See McCrindle's *Ancient India: Its Invasion by Alexander the Great,* p. 169. The following note is given by McCrindle: "According to Stobaeus (who flourished probably at the beginning of the 6th century), an Indian embassy came to Syria in the reign of Antoninus of Emesa (Elagabalus) who reigned from A.D. 218-222. The chief of this embassy Dandamis or Sandanes, having in Mesopotamia met with Bardesanes (flourished in the later half of the 2nd century and perhaps the earlier half of the third), communicated to him information regarding the Indian Gymnosophists which Bardesanes embodied in a work now lost, but of which the following fragment has been preserved by Stobaeus from Porphyry." The story toid by Stobacus, though full of circumstantial details, seems to be somewhat legendary.
30. McCrindle's *Ancient India: Its Invasion by Alexander the Great,* p. 71.
31. *Ibid*, pp. 61, 171. According to the Jainas, one who professed 'angavidyā' was not to be called a Brahmana (*Uttaradhyayana,* Lec. xi—Jacobi's *Jaina Sutras,* ii, S.B.E., p. 341). The practice of medicine is condemned as one of the low arts by the Buddhists (*Mahāparinibbāna Suttanta,* 27). Knowledge of astronomy is essentialloy necessary for a Brahmin. In the Jaina *Uttaradhyayana,* Lec. xxv, 7, 8, the knowledge of Jyotishānga is included among the necessary qualification of a sacrificial priest. (*Jai. Su*., ii, p. 137). But astronomical observations are included in the low arts in the *Mahāparinibbāna Suttanta*, 24.
32. Munis are described as Vātarasanāh or wind-clad in *Rig-Veda,* X. 136, 2.

33. Vihāre vijjamāne * * * sulabha-dassanam dassanakāmānam anikete duddasanā bhavissantī ti (Tenckner's *Milindapanho,* p. 212).

34. *E.g.*, Yathā mahārāja dipika aranne tinagahanam vā vanagahanam vā nissāya nilīyitvā mige gamhāti, evam eva kho mahārāja yoginā yogāvacarena vivekam sevitabbam, etc..... vasībhāvam pāpunāti—*Ibid*, p. 369. This is quoted only as a typical passage.

35. See Cullavagga, VI, 3.10.

36. See Mahavagga, VI, 15.2.

37. See Mahavagga, I, 73.4. See also description of the stately Vihara built by Udayi in the forest—*Suttavibhanga,* Sangh, II, 1.1: also Vihāra built for Palita in a forest—Commentary on *Dhammapada* (P.T.S.), p. 85, 1.13.

38. Sītam unham patihanti tato vālamigani ca

Sirimsape ca makase ca sisire cāpi vutthiyo,

Tato vatātapo ghoro sanjāto patihannati

Lenaṭṭhan ca sukhatthan ca jhāyitum ca vipassitum,

Vihāradānam samghassa aggam buddhen vanninam

Tasmā hi pandito poso sampassam attham attano

Vihāra kāraye ramme vāsayettha hahussute.

Cullavagga, VI, 1.5.

39. *Vinaya Texts,* Pt. II, p. 386, footnote.

40. *The Rock-cut Tempers of India*(1864), Intro., pp. xv-xvi.

41. Cullavagga, VI, 1.4.

42. *E.g.*, 'Vihārena vihāram parivenena parivenam upasamkamitvā Bhikkhū pucchati' (Mahavagga, VI, 36.4); "mama vihāro mama parivenam' (Fausböll's *Dhammapada,* p. 281). See other examples given by Childers under Parivenam in his *Dictionary of the Pali Language.*

43. See Mahavagga, I, 25.14, *et. seq.*

44. See Mahavagga, III, 5.8, etc.

45. Mahavagga, II, 8.1.

46. *Ibid*, II, 8.2.

47. *Ibid*, II, 9.1

48. *Gautama*, III, 13; *Baudhāyana,* II, 6, 11, 20. Haradatta explains ध्रुवशीलो वर्षासु in *Gautama,* as ध्रुवशीलः स्यादेकव तिष्ठेदिति । We are not told whether the Bhikkhu was to live alone or in company during this period.

49. See *Jaina Sutras,* Pt. I, pp. 296-311 (Rules for Yatis).

50. *Ibid.*, pp. 296-97.

51. Mahavagga III, 2.2. See Rhys Davids and Oldenberg's note thereon in *Vinaya Texts,* Pt. I, p. 303, footnote 1.

52. The tropical rains may have been more formidable in the 7th, 6th and 5th centuries, B.C. in Northern India when large tracts were covered with jungles.

53. Per Edward Clodd in the *Story of the Primitive Man*, p. 36.

54. II, 22.

55. Cullavagga, VI, 11.3: anujānāmi bhikhhave vassānam temāsam patibāhitum utukālam no patibāhitum ti.

56. Mahavagga, II, 6.

57. *Ibid.*, II, 7.1. and 2.

58. *Ibid.*, II, 12.7.

59. *Ibid.*, *supra*.

60. *Ibid.*, II, 13.1-2.

61. *Ibid.*, II, 23.

62. *Ibid.*, II, 24.2.

63. *Ibid.*, II, 24, 2., *e.g.*, 'na tu eva vaggena samghena uposatha kātabbo. Kāreyya ce, āpatti dukkatassa.'

64. Mahavagga, VIII, 32.

65. See Mahavagga, VIII, 32.1. (mātikā, No. 2).

66. See Mahavagga, VII, 13. (The two *Palibodhas* are Cīvara and Āvāsa.

67. See Mahavagga, IV, 15. 4.

68. See *Dialogues of Buddha,*Vol. III, p. 255.

69. The following inscriptions for instance which are all taken from the Stupas of Amaravati (Report of the *Archæological Survey of Southern India,* Vol. I, 1883):

(*i*) *Vinayadhirasa* Aya-Punavasusa atevasinaya—
Of the female disciple of Aya-p., the Vinayadhara on Professor of Vinaya—p. 37 (No. 8).

(*ii*) Sidha Odiparivenena vasikasa *dhamakathikasa* Budhi—Of Budhi the Dhammakathaka, etc., p. 94 (No. 3).

(*iii*) ....liyanam *mahavinayadharasa* Aya-Budhisa pavachi (ta)—Of the pupil of Aya-Budhi the Mahavinayadhara, p. 102 (No. 25).

Of them, (*ii*) is in Maurya characters and must be very, very ancient. The other titles also may be found elsewhere. Of such names Rhys Davids says: "They specify an occupation (as we might say, John the Carpenter or John the Clerk)." *Buddhist India,* p. 167.

70. *E.g.*, the 'mythological Suttas' (*e.g., Janavasabha Suttanta*) translated in the *Dialogues of Buddha*, Vol. III. In the Suttanta just named, in the last paragraph of 28 and in 29, emphasis is laid on the eternity of Buddha's religion which is derived in 29 thus; Brahma Sanatkumara > Vessanvana > Janavasabha > Tathāgata > Ānanda > Buddhist monks and laymen > Mankind in general.

71. *E.g.*, the story of Dīghāvū in Mahāvagga, X, 2.2-20; the beast-fable in Cullavagga, VI, 6.3. No identification with a previous incarnation of Buddha is made in these fables.

72. See Tylor's *Primitive Culture,* Vol. II (1891), pp. 11 ff.
73. See Rhys Davids's *Buddhist India,* p. 142.
74. Mahavagga, IX, 4.2.
75. *Ibid.*, IX, 4.7.
76. Cullavagga, VI, 11.3.
77. Mahavagga, I!, 35.4.
78. Cullavagga, II, 1.3.
79. See Cullavagga, XII, 2.8.
80. See *Journal of the Buddhist Text Society of Calcutta,*Vol. I, Pt. III, p. 18; Rhys Davids's article on the *Buddhist Sects* in J.R.A.S., 1891, pp. 411 ff. and 1892, pp. 1-37, and Takakasu's *I-Tsiang*, Intro., pp. xxiii-xxv.
81. Some light is thrown on the two sects, Pubbaseliya and Aparaseliya, by the Amaravati inscriptions. The two sects originated in the two famous cave-vihāras of Dhanakataka. Not far from Dhanakataka was Sanchi, the old name of which was Cetiyagiri. It was even in the pre Asokan age a flourishing seat of Buddhism (see Rhys Davids's *Buddhist India,* p. 286). It seems that a sect was formed here called Cetiyavāda. In the Amarāvati inscriptions, the Cetiyavāda school is frequently mentioned. See *Report of the Archæological Survey of Southern India,* Vol. I, 1883, pp. 100-101). Rhys Davids says: "The Cetiyavada school was very probably the source of the 'schools of the Eastern and Western caves at Dhanakataka, as its name occurs once on the Amaravati tope in the description of one of the donors, a member of the order, resident in one or other of these mountain vihāras" (*Sects of the Buddhists,* J.A.S.B., 1891, footnote).
82. Nāyyo ete bhikkhū paribbājakā' ti—Cullavagga, V, 23.2; *cf.* also Pācittiya, 41: Yo pana bhikkhu acelakassa vā paribbājakassa vā paribbājikāya vā sahatthā khādanīyam vā bhojanīyam vā dadeyya, pācittiyam. In the *Suttavibhanga,* loc passim, 'paribbajaka' is said to be any person other than a Bhikkhu or Sramanera.
83. See Boissonada's Text of *Barlaam and Josaphat* in *Anecdota Graeca,* translated in part by Robert Chalmers in the *'Parables of Barlaam and Josaphat* in J.R.A.S., 1891: "When monasteries commenced to spring up in Egypt and monks to assemble in great numbers and when the report of their virtue and angelic life * * * came to the Indians, it aroused these latter also to a like zeal, so that many of them leaving all took to the wilderness."
84. For a summary account of Egyptian monachism, sèe *Cambridge Medieval History*, Vol. I, Chapter on *Monasticism* (pp. 521-26).
85. See *ibid.*, p. 522.
86. See *ibid.*, p. 524.

6

The Internal Polity of a Buddhist Sangha

The laws of polity by which the early Buddhist Sanghas were governed betray a remarkable maturity of development. They must have passed through many stages before reaching that completeness and perfection which characterise them in the Vinayapitaka. Many of these legal institutions did not surely originate and develop in the Buddhist Sangha itself. There must have been borrowing and adaptation, for, as Humboldt has truly said, 'Man ever connects on from what lies at hand.' A detached study of Buddhist institutions of monastic government apart from their external connections would therefore necessarily lead to an imperfect unhistorical view. As Tylor has said, "It is always unsafe to detach a custom from its hold on past events treating it as an isolated fact to be simply disposed of by some plausible explanation."[1] The general background of primitive Paribrajaka life together with the state-polities of the ancient Indians should therefore be explored in order to discover, if possible, the origins of these institutions. But the inadequacy of materials for this line of research is a great handicap, as will be explained in the next two paragraphs.

The leading note of early Buddhist polity, as we shall see, was that of republican Church Government. If it could be ascertained how far it was characteristic of the other contemporary Paribrajaka sects it would give us a clearer insight into this peculiarity of the constitution of a Buddhist Sangha. It has been observed in a previous chapter that each Sangha or Gana of Paribrajakas in the 6th century B.C., had a recognised leader or Satthā, as he was called. Whether a line of succession would inevitably follow or some other kind of organisation would come into existence on the death of the first Satthā is an obscure question, the complete and satisfactory solution of which is impossible in the absence of more abundant materials than we now possess. We have indeed brief and scrappy sketches of the doctrines of some Paribrajaka sects in the Sāmanna-phala Sutta.[2] Of these sects, our knowledge of the Ājīvakas is supplemented by other sources. They are many scattered references to them in Buddhist and Jaina literatures, supplying for the most part little useful information. Besides there are two systematic treatments of the Ājīvaka doctrines from the Buddhist and the Jaina points of view respectively in the Sumangala-Vilāsini by Buddhaghosa[3] and in the 6th Ajjayana of Uvāsagadasāo.[4] In the 15th Sataka of the Bhagavati Sutta[5] again we have a legendary account of the life of the founder of the Ājīvaka sect, much garbled though it is by religious prejudice. But the Jaina and Buddhist writers are naturally more intent on refuting their doctrines than giving anything like an historical account of them, and the result is that though we know something about the peculiar 'dhamma' of Gosāla, we are totally in the dark about the character or organisation of the Sangha or Gana which he founded. The subsequent history of the Ājīvakas tempts but baffles enquiry, though their existence in the 3rd century, B.C. is indicated by the mention of them in a few well-known inscription.[6]

The records of the Jainas give us a better, though by no means satisfactory, view of the early organisation of their Order. The enumeration of the Ganas, Kulas and Sākhās in the Sthavirāvalī cannot of course be regarded as historical in the absence of other evidence. But it is important and significant as showing that the 'republican-idea' did not prevail among the early Jaina community. "It is not quite clear, quite clear," says Jacobi, "what is meant by Gana, Kula and Sākhā. Gana designates the school which is derived from one teacher; Kula the succession of teachers in one line; Sākhā the line which branched off from one teacher. These terms seem to be disused in modern times, for the four principal divisions called after Nagendra, Chandra, Nivritti, and Vidyādhara are generally called Kulas, but also occasionally Sākhās. They go back to

Vajra, according to some, to Vajrasena, according to others. The modern Gaccha appears equivalent with the ancient Gana."[7] In the organisation of the Buddhist community, however, as reflected in the Pitakas, this principle of ruling hegemony is conspicuous by its absence. In the Jaina *Rules for Yatis,* it is said, for instance, "As the venerable ascetic, Mahāvīrā, commenced the Pajjusan when a month and twenty nights of the rainy season had elapsed, so the Ganadharas commenced the Pajjusan when a month and twenty nights of the rainy season had elapsed. As the Ganadharas have done, so the disciples of the Ganadharas have done. As they have done, so the Sthaviras have done. As they have done, so do the Nirgrantha Sramanas of the present time."[8] It would be difficult to cite a parallel passage from the Vinayapitaka. In early Buddhism in fact, the idea of a succession of teachers is definitely rejected, though it managed to edge itself into it later on. In the Introduction to the Samantapāsādikā, Buddhagosha names a succession of teachers (ācariya-paramparā) from Upali to Tisso, who handed down the Vinaya to the third Synod,[9] *viz.*,

Upāli Dāsako c' eva Sonaka Siggavo tathā
Tisso Moggaliputto ca panc' ete vijitāvino
Paramparāya Vinayam dīpe Jambusirivhaye
Acchijjamānam ānesum tatiyo yāva samgaho' ti.

The sense in which Buddhaghosha uses the word, ācariya, here is unknown to the Vinayapitaka.[10] Upali who stands at the head of the list is nowhere represented in early Buddhist literature as occupying any permanent official position as the Vinaya-teacher of the Sangha; he was selected only for the occasion at the first Council to recite the Vinaya, being most learned in it, being a Vinayadhara. Buddhaghosa's Ācariya-paramparā (which is elaborated in later Buddhist literature), even if it may be regarded as analogous to the Jaina Sthavirāvalī, is a much later idea, absent in early Buddhist literature and evolved most probably by Buddhaghosa himself in the 5th century, A.D.[11] It can throw no light on the ideas of polity of the early Buddhist Sanghas.

The transition of the Sangha, after the death of the first Satthā 'from a monarchical to a republican type'[12] as Oldenberg felioitously puts it, seems therefore to be rather peculiar—no analogous idea being found in Jainism and none surely in Hinduism. Of the Ājīvakas and other sects, we know next to nothing on this point. On the idea of a succession of masters the canonical literature of the Buddhists is far from being silent. It is likely that the question was agitated among the Bhikkhus in early times and the emphasis with which it is answered may have been due to its having been seriously propounded at some time. In Cullavagga, VII, 3.1, Devadatta proposes to Buddha that as he has grown old and is near the end of his life, he (Buddha) should hand over the leadership of the Sangha to him (Jinno dāni bhante bhagavā,* * * mama bhikkhusangham nissajjatu, aham bhikkhusangham pariharissāmīti). But Buddha retorts with the reply that he would not hand over the leadership of the Sangha even to Sariputta or Moggallana, much less to an evil person like him. In the Mahāparinibbāna Sutta,[13] Ananda expresses the hope that the Tathāgata will before his decease leave some instructions regarding the Sangha (na tāva bhagavā parinibbāyissati na yāva bhagavā bhikkhusangham ārabbha kincid eva udāharatīti). Buddha in his reply strongly repudiates the idea of a successor to him leading the Sangha and his words are intensely emphatic—Atta-dīpā viharatha atta-saranā ananna-saranā dhamma-dīpā dhamma-saranā aranna-saranā. Buddha even goes so far as to say—"Tathāgatassa kho Ānanda na evam hoti 'Aham bhikkhu-sangham pariharissāmīti' vā 'Mam uddesiko bhikkhusaṅgho' ti vā." The inconsistency of this with another statement made by Assaji has already been noticed. The obvious explanation is that the idea that there was no leader of the Sangha, no one on whom the Sangha was dependent, came to the fore after the death of the first master (Satthā), and this later idea is put into the mouth of the Buddha in the Mahāparinibbāna Sutta. No successor to the original Satthā was recognised. This is made more clear in Mahāparinibbāna Sutta, VI, 1.1: "Siyā kho pan Ānanda tumhākam evam assa: atītasatthukam pāvacanam, n'athi no satthā ti. Na kho pan' etam Ānanda evam datthabbam, yo vo

Ānanda mayā dhammo ca vinayo ca desito pannatto so vo mam' accayena satthā" This is further elucidated in the Gopaka-Moggallāna Suttanta in the Majjhima Nikaya[14] where Vassakara asks Ananda whether Gotama has marked out any particular Bhikkhu who should be the refuge of the Sangha after his death. Ananda answers in the negative. Vassakara then asks whether any one has been subsequently nominated in that behalf. Being answered in the negative, he asks how unity can exist among the followers of Gotama. Ananda answers, "There is no want to us of a refuge, O Brahmana! we have a refuge, the Dhamma." Evidently the republican organisation of the Buddhist Sangha was somewhat incomprehensible to outsiders.

When, in course of time, the original Cātuddisa Bhikkhusangha had broken up into several monastic communities (sanghas) belonging to different āvāsas, the 'republican idea' was consistently maintained. In an early Buddhist Sangha there was no one answering to an 'abbot'. One who aspired to such a position in an āvāsa was condemned as a fool.[15] For the conduct of the affairs of the Sangha—its trials, deliberations and other business—a learned and virtuous person among the community would be appointed president. But his character was strictly representative. "If he is charged with a mission, he takes it upon himself properly, and in the business of the Sangha, he does what they tell him;—when a number of Bhikkhus despatches him somewhere he obeys their command, but he does not think thereupon, 'It is I who do this'" (Dūteyyakammesu alam samuggaho sanghassa kiccesu ca āhunam yathā, Karamavaco bhikkhuganena pesito aham karomīti na tena mannati).[16] It is said of Lanfranc that he used to read 'e' in 'Docēre' short at the bidding of his ignorant superior.[17] Such an incident would be inconceivable in a Buddhist Sangha. The point as to whether the Upajjhāya or Ācariya should be unquestioningly followed was raised at the Council of Vesali and was ruled out. (Cullavagga, XII, 1.10—Acinnakappa). There is no place for such obedience as is insisted on, say, in the *Regula Benediciti*[18] in the whole of the Vinayapitaka.

Deference is limited to respectful attention to seniors, apportioning of the best seats, water and food according to seniority, not taking the same seat with a senior, etc.[19] It is this kind of courteous and attentive deference to superiors and elders that is recommended in the Mahāparinibbāna Suttanta, 1, 6., *e.g.*, Yāvakīvan ca bhikkhave bhikkhū ye te bhikkhū therā ratannū cirapabbajitā sangha-pitaro sangha-parināyakā te sakkarissanti gurukarissanti mānessanti pūjessanti tesan ca sotabbam mannissanti vuddhi yeva bhikkhave bhikkhūnam pātikankhā no parihāni.

The idea of the paramount authority of a person—a recognised head, a spiritual dictator, an abbot or a *gana dhara*—was foreign to the republican constitution of an early Buddhist Sangha. The republican church government of the early Buddhists seems to be somewhat striking in its originality. But the fact must not be forgotten that the political constitution of many tribes of north-eastern India in early times whence Buddhist Bhikkhu were largely recruited was of a republican type.[20] People were quite familiar and conversant with free institutions like voting, committee, popular tribunal and collective legislation, and if many of them were readily transplanted in the constitution of the Buddhist Sangha, there would be nothing surprising or unnatural in the fact. Mr. K.P. Jayaswal has hazarded the conjecture that "the Buddhist brotherhood, the Sangha, was copied out from the political Sangha, the republic, in its constitution."[21] But this remains a conjecture only, though by no means an improbable one, in the present state of our knowledge. As we have said above, our knowledge of the constitution and organisation of other contemporary sects of Paribrajakas, which might probably have influenced the Buddhist Sangha, is extremely defective.

A primitive āvāsa was a republican colony of Buddhist Bhikkhus as directly democratic in its constitution as any city-state of ancient Greece. The Government was based on universal suffrage and every duly qualified member had an equal right of participating in it. Any transaction of the monastic community which might affect the Sangha in any way was called a Sanghakamma. There were various forms of Sanghakamma, a classified list of the more important of which is given below:—

Sanghakamma

I Disciplinary and Disputatious		II Non-disciplinary and Non-disputatious	III Anomalous
	(*a*) Apatichanna	1. pasampadā	1. Tassa- Pāpiyyasika
	(*b*) Patichanna	2. Uposatha	2. Tina-vitthāraka
1. Parivāsa	(*c*) Suddhanta or Mulāya Patikassanā	3. Settlement of Sīmā	
	(*d*) Samodhāna	4. Pavāranā	
2. Mānatta		5. Kanthina	
3. Tajjaniya		6. Appointment of all officers	
4. Nissaya		7. Dedication of any part of the building establishment for any special purpose.	
5. Pabbājaniya			
6. Patisāraniya	Patta-Nikkujana (its counter-part)	8. Settlement of succession to the personal belongings of any deceased Bhikkhu.	
	(*a*) Āpattiyā Adassane		
7. Ukkhepaniya	(*b*) Āpattiyā Appatikamme	9. Abbhāna	
	(*c*) Papikāya Ditthiyā Appatinissagge		
8. Pakāsaniya			*Et cetera*
9. Brahmadanda			

In Class I, Nos. (1), (2) and (9) were probably older than the rest. The first two forms of discipline to be imposed by the Sangha are the only ones mentioned and described in the Pātimokkha. No. (9) is described only in the *Mahāparinibbāna Sutta*. Nos. (3)—(7) seem to have been the regular and ordinary forms. They could not be resorted to without previous confession on the part of the guilty Bhikkhu (Cullavagga, IV, 7.1). They are explained and elaborated in Cullavagga, I. No. (8) seems to have been an exceptional form and there is no reference to it except in the story of Devadatta on whom it was imposed. It is likely that other forms of discipline besides those enumerated in the above list could be invented to suit occasions. In Class II, No. (1) became a Sanghakamma only later on. It passed through three formal stages—Ehi Bhikkhu, Saranāgama and Kammavācā. (See Chapter VII). In Class III, Nos. (1) and (2) are called Forms of Procedure (Adhikaranasamattha), but they have all the characteristics of Sanghakamma proper. Vijesinha expresses this opinion with regard to No. (1) (See Childers's *Pali Dictionary, loc. cit*).

I am solely responsible for the above classified list. The division of Sanghakammas into these three classes is not based on any orthodox authority. But it seems to me to be the only reasonable classification possible. The significance of the three heads of Sanghakammas will, I believe be clearer on a perusal of the whole of this chapter.

For the transaction of a Sanghakamma, it would be necessary to assemble together the *whole* Sangha. Any one not able to join in it must either remain outside the boundary of the āvāsa or send his consent through another which was called Chanda.[22] The completeness of the assembly is insisted on, and in the Mahāparinibbāna Sutta one of the safeguards against the degeneration of the Sangha is said to be the holding of *complete* assemblies for the purpose of transacting Sanghakammas.[23] A complete assembly for the purpose of the various Sanghakammas is defined as one consisting of:—[24]

(*i*) Four—for all acts except Upasampadā, Pavāranā and Abbhāna.

(*ii*) Five—for all acts except Upasampadā in border countries, and Abbhāna. ("In such Border Countries, I allow, O Bhikkhus, the Upasampadā to be held in a meeting of only four Bhikkhus besides the Chairman who must be a Vinayadhara"—Mahavagga, V, 13.12; For the boundaries, see *ibid*).

(*iii*) Ten—for all acts except Abbhāna.

(*iv*) Twenty and upwards for all acts.

It is to be understood that these minima would constitute quorums, but not committees. The boundaries for example of an āvāsa have got to be settled. Three Bhikkhus are present. They may not transact business unless another Bhikkhu turns up and helps to form the quorum. Suppose now only four Bhikkhus are present. They may validly transact the business. Suppose again seven Bhikkhus are present. They may transact business only if *all* of them join in it: it would not be competent for four of them to transact the business apart from the remaining three, that is, by a committee. A committee is recognised only in one case, *viz.*, the Ubbāhikā form of procedure. The right of direct participation in the Sanghakamma inheres in each duly qualified member of an āvāsa and is very jealously guarded.

Again, the minimum number must not be made up by any person under any of the twenty-four disabilities mentioned in Mahavagga, IX, 4.2. Two of them deserve special mention, *viz.*, (*i*) living outside the boundary (nānāsimāya thita) and (*ii*) belonging to a different āvāsa (nānāsamvāsaka). That these two conditions were of later imposition is suggested by the following significant inconsistency. In Mahavagga, III, 6-9, certain exceptional cases are contemplated regarding Vassa residence. During the sojournment of the rain-retreat, a Bhikkhu at an āvāsa, for instance, desires Parivāsa, Mānatta or Abbhāna, but owing to the shortage of the minimum number, according to the rules stated above, the Sanghakamma cannot be transacted. He invites a Bhikkhu to come from outside and become a Ganapūraka, *i.e.*, help to make up the requisite number. The outsider is permitted, as an exceptional case, to leave his own place of residence during the Vassa and go to the place where he is wanted. Now such an outsider would be either under disability, No. 21 (nānāsamvāsaka) or No. 22 (nānāsīmāya thita). How could he act as a Ganapūraka without contravening the provision of Mahavagga, IX, 4.2, *et. seq.*? The fact is that the idea of the distinctness of each āvāsa developed gradually as pointed out in the previous chapter and the rules, Nos. 21 and 22, must be read in the light of the history of the growth of the āvāsas.

The form of a Sanghakamma consisted of two parts—first, Natti (Resolution) and then, Anussāvanā (Proclamation of the proposed act or Kammavācā).[25] The inversion of this order would invalidate the whole proceedings *ab initio*.[26] The matter for decision by Sanghakamma was defined by a Bhikkhu in the form of a Resolution placed before the whole assembly—'Let this (the matter defined) be done.' Then followed the Proclamation. Those who were against the Resolution were called upon to speak and those who were for it to remain silent. This Proclamation might be made only once when the act was called a Nattidutiya Kamma or thrice when it was a Natticatuttha Kamma. Some Sanghakammas belonged to the first order and some to the second and the observance of this distinction was essential for the validity of an act.

To sum up, the following would be the essential conditions of a valid act:[27]

(*i*) The presence of the minimum number competent to perform the act. This was a condition precedent. In other words ratification (anumati) by a member who was not actually present at the Sanghakamma given after it had been performed was invalid. This was decided at the Council of Vesali (Cullavagga, XII, 1. 10.)

(*ii*) The consent of all the absentees conveyed by Chanda.

(*iii*) The proposal of the Resolution (Natti).

(*iv*) The proclamation of Kammavācā (Anussāvana), once or thrice, according as the act was of the Nattidutiya or of the Natticatuttha class.

(*v*) Consent to the proposal given by silence of all duly qualified members of the assembly. When there was a division of opinion, it became a case of Adhikarana (Dispute) which must be settled as *per* rules explained below.

The failure to satisfy any of these conditions would invalidate the act. When the act was invalid it might be impugned at another assembly by way of a Kiccādhikarana, and the matter opened afresh. But when the matter was decided by a valid act, it became *res judicate* and the reopening of it would amount to Pācittiya offence, No. 63.[28]

Now a Sanghakamma might arise in either of the two following ways—(*i*) by a general requisition and (*ii*) through a dispute. Non-disciplinary Sanghakammas would generally arise in the first way. When the sense of the whole Sangha was understood to be in favour of a particular measure, it was brought formally before the Sangha and carried through by regular proposal and proclamation. When on the other hand the sense of the Sangha was divided, it became a case of (*ii*). It is obvious that all disciplinary Sanghakammas would belong to this latter class, for in them the rest of the Bhikkhus acted against a single or a number of Bhikkhus. But nevertheless with a few specified exceptions there might be a division on almost any matter. With regard to this latter class of Sanghakammas, arising by way of dispute, the proceedings were somewhat special, consisting of the following stages:

(*i*) The *Dispute* (Preliminary to the trial):

(*a*) Accusation and denial; or

(*b*) Confession of guilt; or

(*c*) Difference of opinion on any of the specified matter.

N.B.—The denial in (*a*), if false, would be a fresh offence leading to Ukkhepanīyakamma (Act of suspension).

(*ii*) The *Procedure* (the trial proper):

(*a*) Proposal of the Resolution (Natti), and

(*b*) Proclamation of Kammavācā, both in accordance with

(*c*) the rules of Adhikaranasamattha.

(*iii*) The *Decision* of the Sangha (Judgment).

Now the difference between the form and procedure of a non-disciplinary and non-disputatious action and that of a disciplinary and disputatious one is this—in the former, the first stage is absent and there are no special rules, as in *ii* (*c*), governing the Natti.

The brief outline sketched above appears to be simple enough, but when we proceed to details, we are confronted with elaborate complications. The whole process of conducting a disputatious Sanghakamma grows into such a tangled labyrinth that unless we thread our way through it with the greatest care and caution we are likely to be 'in wandering mazes lost.' I shall however try to set out the details of the process as clearly and simply as accuracy of presentment would allow.

To commence from the first stage. Disputes or Adhikaranas are divided into 4 classes according to the subject-matter of the dispute, *viz.*,[29]

(*i*) *Vivādadhikarena*—Dispute on certain specified matters which may be summarised as (*a*) Dhamma, (*b*) Vinaya, (*c*) the teachings, practices or ordainments of the Tathāgata, (*d*) the nature of an ecclesiastical offence. Disputes on these matters would tend to give rise to schisms (see Cullavagga, VII, 5.2).

Exceptions.—Friendly and family disputes are excepted.[30]

(*ii*) *Anuvādādhikarana*—Dispute regarding the state of a Bhikkhu's opinion, morals, character, conduct or manner of life.

Exceptions—Friendly and family disputes are excepted.[30]

(*iii*) *Āpattādhikarana*—Dispute regarding the following kinds of offences, *viz.*, Pārājika, Sanghādisesa, Pācittiya, Pātidesaniya, Dukkata, Thullaccaya and Dubbāsita, alleged against any Bhikkhu.

Exceptions—Anything whatever called an Āpatti (*e.g.*, so t-āpatti, sam-āpatti, etc.) is not necessarily the subject of an āpattādhikarana.

N.B.—It will be observed that when the Bhikkhu had been guilty of an offence, which could not be brought under any of the above heads, the allegation of it against him would not give rise to an Āpattādhikarana, but an Anuvādādhikarana which is much more comprehensive in its scope.

(*iv*) *Kiccādhikarana*—Dispute regarding the procedure of a Sanghakamma or the duties and obligations of the Sangha.

Exceptions—The duties of an ācariya, an upajjhāya or a fellow-pupil could not be the subject of a Kiccādhikarana.

The following illustrations may be taken of the above four classes:—

(*i*) At an āvāsa in Vesali, some Bhikkhus invite laymen to offer money to the Sangha: Yasa says that it is against the Dhamma—this is a Vivādādhikarana which must be formally brought before the Sangha. (See account of the Council of Vesali in Cullavagga, XII, 1).

(*ii*) At an āvāsa in Vesali, some Bhikkhus allege that Yasa has propounded a false doctrine to laymen—this is an Anuvādādhikarana which must be formally brought before the Sangha (see *ibid.*).

(*iii*) At an āvāsa in Rajagaha, a Bhikkhuni named Mettiyā complains that Dabba has committed the 6th Pācittiya offence against her—this is an Āpattādhikarana which must be formally brought before the Sangha. (See the story of Dabba in Cullavagga, IV, 4.8.)

(*iv*) At an āvāsa, X alleges that a certain Sanghakamma has not been attended with the necessary conditions, *e.g.*, the minimum number was not made up—this is a Kiccādhikarana which must be formally brought before the Sangha.

So much about the dispute itself.

At the second stage, the Adhikarana has been brought before the full assembly. In a non-disciplinary and non-disputatious Sanghakamma, the Natti at this stage would be put without further preliminaries. But not so in the other Sanghakammas. The person concerned—the prisoner at the bar, as modern lawyers would say—must submit to certain interrogatories on the result of which the Natti—whether of acquittal or of conviction—would be put. The accused would be called upon to remember his offence or warned or made to confess, etc.

There are various technical terms, *e.g.*, codetabba (as in Sammukhavinaya), āpattim āropetabba (as in Amulhavinaya), etc., to signify different forms of interrogatories. When the result of the interrogatories had been known, it would be time to put the Natti which would be governed by the rules of the Adhikaranasamattha.[31] These rules, governing the Natti, are seven in number of which the last two, as I have already remarked, are somewhat different in character from the rest, *viz.*, (*i*) Sammukhavinaya, (*ii*) Sativinaya, (*iii*) Patinnātakarana, (*iv*) Amulhavinaya, (*v*) Jebhuyyasikā, (*vi*) Tassa-pāpiyasikā, (*vii*) Tinavitthāraka. Of these rules one or two combined would apply under different sets of circumstances to be explained below, No. (*i*) being common to all. We now proceed to consider these circumstances under which the rules would apply.[32]

(*i*) Sammukhavinaya—This means the presence (*a*) of the particular individual concerned, (*b*) of the Sangha or the full assembly, (*c*) of the Vinaya (which means the observance of the proper rules of procedure), and (*d*) of the Dhamma (which means the application of the law relating to the case). This 'fourfold presence' applies to *all* adhikaranas. It safeguards the proper conduct of the trial. There are two exceptional forms of Sammukhavinaya—(*a*) Reference to the members of another āvāsa and (*b*) Reference to a committee of the same āvāsa duly appointed. In the case of (*a*), if the referees were unable to decide the question, the custody of the case was returned by them. The following rules would govern (*b*): A committee (Ubbāhikā) would be appointed when in the course of the proceedings confusion arose and the assembly found it impossible to come to a decision. The members of the committee would be appointed in the usual Natti-form by which all office-bearers of the Sangha were appointed. The rules according to which the committee itself would proceed to consider the business before it are not laid down. But in the account of the Council at Vesali where such a committee was appointed, the procedure of the committee is represented as follows[33]: The committee consists of 8 members. One of them, Sabbakāmi, acts like a Chairman and another, Revata, acts like a Secretary.

The points referred to the Committee are put one by one by the Secretary to the Chairman, and as each point is decided by the latter, the Secretary announces it to the other members of the Committee and casts the ballot accordingly (*cf.* Idam pathamam salākam nikkhipāmi—Cullavagga, XII, 2. 8). When all the points are decided the Chairman tells the Secretary that the matter is settled an concluded once for all, but that he (Secretary) should nevertheless interrogate him (Chairman) in the midst of the whole Sangha on all the points over again. This is accordingly done which brings the whole proceedings relative to the case to a termination. If however the committee found it impossible to decide the matter delegated to it, the custody of the case was re-transferred to the Sangha and it was then settled by the Sangha according to the Jebhuyyasikā form of Adhikaranasamattha, *i.e.*, by the vote of the majority.

(*ii*) Sativinaya—When a person had been accused of any misconduct and he, being clearly conscious of his innocence, repudiated the charge, this form was observed. The accused appeared before the Sangha in an attitude of supplication and asked for a discharge in accordance with the Sativinaya form. Then followed the usual Natti in terms of the request preferred, and so on. There must be five requisite conditions for a Sativinaya—(*a*) The accused Bhikkhu must be innocent, (*b*) he must notwithstanding have been charged with the offence of which he pleads not guilty, (*c*) he must have asked the Sangha for a discharge, (*d*) the Sangha must be prepared to grant it, and (*e*) the Sangha must be duly constituted.

(*iii*) Patinnātakarana—When a Bhikkhu, guilty of a slight offence (lahuka āpatti), pleaded guilty of it, this form was observed. Here the case need not necessarily be carried to the Natti-stage. The guilty Bhikkhu might approach another Bhikkhu or a number of Bhikkhus in the usual attitude of supplication and obtain a valid absolution on confession. If not, he had to appear before the Sangha and made a confession on which the usual Natti, etc., followed and the confessing Bhikkhu was let off with a warning. It should be noted here that the granting of absolution was an act for an individual and not for the collective body. It was not the Sangha that granted absolution, but the person who proposed the Natti. It was only in the form called Tina-vitthāraka that absolution was sought from and granted by the Sangha itself. The principle seems to be that an individual's offence is absolved by an individual or a number of individuals while the offence of the whole Sangha can be absolved by the Sangha itself.

(*iv*) Amulhavinaya—When a person had been accused of an offence committed during insanity, and either (*a*) he fully confessed it, or (*b*) he could not remember it owing to lapse of memory, or (*c*) he continued in an insane state of mind, this form was observed. The procedure was exactly as in Sativinaya.

(*v*) Jebhuyyasikā—This form was adopted only in a Vivādādhikarana and only when the matter in issue was of a grave character (Cullavagga, IV, 10.1) and the assembly got out of hand and a unanimous decision was found to be impossible of achievement. This decision was arrived at by the vote of the majority. The voting was done by means of the distribution of marked pieces of wood called Salāka which were subsequently counted and the majority ascertained thereby. The polling officer was therefore called Salākagāhāpaka. He was appointed in the usual Natti-form like all other office-bearers of the Sangha. A person of unimpeachable honesty and impartiality who was conversant with the rules of procedure would be appointed to this post, for it carried with it a heavy responsibility—the Salākagāhāpaka having power to reject the whole voting if in this view the opinion of the majority was contrary to the Dhamma. When the Salākagāhāpaka had been appointed, he proceeded to his work in either of the three following ways: he might call upon the Bhikkhus to take away the marked Salākas, telling each one as he came up the significance of the marks and asking him to keep his ballot secret (this was thẹ Gulhaka or secret method); or he might whisper the same thing into the ear of each Bhikkhu, probably going round the assembly (this was the Sakannajappaka or whispering method); or, lastly, he might dispense with all secrecy in voting (this was the Vivataka or open method). This last method was adopted when it was known to the Salākagāhāpaka that the vote of the majority would be on the side of the Dhamma. Further details, which may be accepted for all they are worth coming as they do from a late source, are supplied by Buddhaghosa.[34] He says that the first method was adopted when the assembly grew unruly (alajjussanna); the second, when the assembly was composed of ignorant or unintelligent members (bālussanna); and the third, when it was orderly and inclined to observe propriety (lajjussanna). The point to be specially noted in the Jebhuyyasikā form is the large discretionary power left to the polling officer, which was probably intended as a safeguard against possible abuses. Buddhaghosa describes in a quaint and somewhat confused manner how the discretionary power of the polling officer was to be exercised.[35] "When (the vote) is improperly taken," says the learned commentator, "it should be taken till a third time (the polling officer), declaring, 'This improperly taken ballot should be taken again.' If even at the third time those against the Dhamma are in a majority, he (the polling officer) should rise (saying), 'To-day is inauspicious; I shall announce it tomorrow.' The ballot should be taken the next day with (lit. looking for) those who were in the right, with a view to discomfiting the unrighteous members. This is secret balloting. In following the whispering method, on the other hand, if any elderly member of the Sangha voted on the side of the unrighteous ones (lit. took the Salāka of the unrighteous ones), this should be said and made known to him, "Venerable Sir, you are great and aged; this does not become you. The ballot of the righteous ones is the other. The ballot should then be shown to him. If he values it, it should be made over to him. But let him not misunderstand it. (Therefore) he should be told, 'Do not make it known to anybody.' The rest (of the procedure) is as laid down." This native commentary of Buddhaghosa unpleasantly reminds us of modern electioneering tactics, but perhaps even in an American state, the polling-officer would not stoop to wire-pulling and canvassing in the manner that Buddhaghosa innocently recommends.

The two remaining Adhikaranasamatthas are essentially Sanghakamma, with this difference only that in an ordinary

Sanghakamma the offence would arise before the trial while in those two cases the offence would arise in the course of the trial.

(*vi*) Tassa-pāpiyyasikā-kamma—When a Bhikkhu in the course of interrogatories at a trial was guilty of obstinacy or prevarication, this form was adopted as a disciplinary measure. After the commission of the offence as above, the usual Natti was proposed and the Bhikkhu sentenced accordingly. If could arise out of an Anuvādādhikarana and perhaps also an Āpattādhikarana.[36] (Cullavagga, IV, 12.1.—The text says that the Bhikkhu must be 'sānuvādo.' This does not necessarily exclude imputation of āpatti. A too narrow interpretation of the word would be somewhat unreasonable, and the translators also seem to realise this when they write, 'when a censure has been set on foot against him.' The circumstances which would lead to T. Pāp might conceivably arise in both kinds of Adhikarana). Confession, as in other disciplinary Sanghakammas, is a necessary pre-condition. The Tassa-pāp from is in fact exactly analogous to Tajjaniya-kamma, the only distinction being, as I have pointed out, that in the former the offence arises in the course of the trial while in the latter it arises before the trial.

(*vii*) Tina-vitthāraka—This is a curious form devised probably for the purpose of avoiding multiplicity of trials. It might so happen that during the sitting of the judicial assembly, quarrels and disputes took place among the assembled Bhikkhus with the result that numerous grounds of complaint sprang up. It would be obviously inconvenient, if not impossible, to take action on each and all of them. Under such circumstances, the Tina-vitthāraka form was adopted. Serious offences (Pārājika and Sanghādisesa *per* Buddhaghosa) and those which concerned the laity however were beyond its province. Confession, as usual, was a necessary pre-condition. The usual Natti was first proposed. Then one representative from each factious party would make a confession offences in general terms. When this was finished, each representative again brought forward the confession by way of Natti and asked for absolution which was granted according to the terms of the prayer.

The following chart will show how the Adhikarana-samatthas were applied in the four kinds of Adhikarana. The Sammukhavinaya, as said already, was common to all four of them:[37]

(*i*) Vivādādhikarana	Sammukha.
	Sammukha. + Jebhuyyasikā.
(*ii*) Anuvādādhikarana	Sammukha. + Sati.
	Sammukha. + Tassa-pāp.
	Sammukha. + Amulha.
(*iii*) Āpattādhikarana	Sammukha. + Patinnātakarana.
	Sammukha. + Tina-vitthāraka.
(*iv*) Kiccādhikarana	Sammukha.

So much about the second stage of the trial.

To proceed to the third and last stage. The decision might be (*i*) by the whole Sangha, or (*ii*) by a committee of the Sangha, or (*iii*) by a number of referees belonging to another Sangha, or lastly, (*iv*) by the vote of the majority of the Sangha. One kind of tribunal could not be substituted for another except under specified circumstances. To take an illustration. Suppose the Sangha failed to come to a unanimous decision. It would not be proper—except in the case of a Vivādādhikarana—to proceed at once to a decision by vote of majority. The case, as it is said, must have run its course (gatigatam hoti—Cullavagga IV, 10.1). The point at issue must first be referred either to a committee of the same āvāsa or a number of referees belonging to another āvāsa. If they gave their decision, the Sangha was bound by it. If they did not, the case was returned to the Sangha to be decided (*i*) by the vote of the majority when it had been returned by the committee, or (*ii*) otherwise, probably by reference to a committee, when it had been returned by referes belonging to another āvāsa. (There is no provision for Jebhuyyasikā when the case is returned by referees).

But the Jebhuyyasikā mode of decision was hedged in with certain restrictions. Trivial matters could not be submitted to it. The polling officer was invested with plenary powers and, after taking the ballot, he might refuse to ratify the result of the voting if he considered that it would necessarily lead or was likely to lead to a schism, or to the victory of the party manifestly in the wrong, or that the votes had not been sincerely given. Under such circumstances he would arrange for another balloting.

Then again the decision must be in the terms of the Natti. The Natti, as we have observed, might be a Natti of acquittal or of discharge, as in Sativinaya, Amulhavinaya, Patinnātakarana and Tinavitthāraka, or one of conviction as in the several forms of disciplinary Sanghakammas. The trial must be for the offence of which the guilty Bhikkhu is formally accused before the Sangha and not for an offence of which he may have confessed himself to be guilty. For example, a Bhikkhu is charged with a Pārājika, but he confesses to a Sanghādisesa; he must be tried for the former and not for the latter offence (Cullavagga, IV, 8)

Let us now illustrate the legal processes described above by citing two hypothetical cases:

(A) *Disciplinary Sanghakamma*

A. a Bhikkhu belonging to an āvāsa at Rajagaha, is detected in the act of kissing a woman. The offence will come under rule 2 of Sanghādisesa—Jo pana bhikkhu otinno viparinatena cittena matugāmena saddhim kāyasamsaggam samāpajjeyya hatthagaham vā benigaham vā annatarassa vā angassa parāmasanam sanghādisesa. The Bhikkhu, A, is accused of the offence by another Bhikkhu, *B*. This is an Āpattādhikarana, and it is duly brought before a full assembly of the Sangha. The accused, A, is now interrogated by another Bhikkhu, *C*. before the whole assembly. Now it is clear that as the offence is not a light one (lahuka āpatti), the accused cannot obtain absolution by confession, and so the form, Sammukha+Patinnātakarana, will not apply. A Natti, either of acquittal or of conviction, will have to be put on the result of the interrogatories. The accused may at this stage take any of the following pleas:—

(*i*) I was out of mind at the time when I committed the offence (plea of insanity).

(*ii*) I do not remember to have committed the offence.

(*iii*) I refuse to make any confession.

(*iv*) I confess to having committed the offence.

(*v*) (The accused confesses and denies, makes a plea and retracts it and so on.)

(*vi*) I have committed no Sanghādisesa offence, but a Pācittiya one (*e.g.*, I did not kiss the woman, Sanghā. 2, but only sat together with her in a solitary place, Pāc. 45)

Suppose he takes the first plea. The assembly may be satisfied with it or not. If satisfied, the accused must request the Sangha, to adopt with regard to him the Amulhavinaya form. A Natti will then be put by another Bhikkhu in terms of the request made and the Anussāvana will follow. The Sangha will then signify by its silence that the accused is dischanged according to Amulhavinaya. If however the Sangha is not satisfied with the plea, there are two courses open to it. Either it may suspend the accused for not atoning for a fault (āpattiyā appatikamme ukkhepaniyakamma), or it may straightway proceed to sentence him to the discipiine of Parivāsa and Mānatta according to the Pātimokkha. (For this disciplinary measure confession is not a necessary pre-condition). In both cases the proper Natti and Anussāvana must be gone through.

The second plea can only be taken by one whose memory may be trusted.[38] The steps are the same as above.

Suppose the accused takes the third plea. There are two courses open to the Sangha—either to suspend the accused for not confessing an offence (āpattiyā adassane ukkhepaniyakamma) or to sentence him according to law. It is obvious that in this case the accused cannot be discharged or acquitted.

Suppose the accused takes the fourth plea. He will then have to approach the assembly in an attitude of humility and, after making the confession, request the Sangha to inflict upon him the Mānatta discipline. A Natti will then be put in terms of the request and Anussāvana will follow, these being repeated three times. The Sangha will signify by its silence that it sentences the accused to the Mānatta discipline of six days' duration. (When the offence is not concealed, the Parivāsa part of the penalty is remitted—Cullavagga, III, 1).

Suppose the accused takes the fifth plea. The plea, if it can be so called at all, may be taken, as I have said already, not only in an Anuvādādhikarana for which it is specially mentioned, but also possibly in an Āpattādhikarana. A Bhikkhu will then put a Natti that owing to his obstinate conduct, the Tassa-pāpiyyasikā Kamma should be carried out against him and Anussāvanā will follow. The Sangha will then signify by its silence that the accused is sentenced accordingly.

Suppose the accused takes the sixth plea. He cannot in that case be dealt with on the basis of his confession. He must either be suspended or be sentenced for the offence of which he is accused and not for that of which he pleads guilty. Under the circumstances, the most prudent thing for the accused to do would be to take the second plea and get a discharge. He may of course be tried afterwards on a proper charge made on the basis of his confession.

(B) *Non-Disciplinary Sanghakamma*

Suppose in the case taken above the Bhikkhu has worked out the sentence and has expressed a desire to be re-instated and the Sangha is ready to comply. Then in order to re-habilitate him, the Sangha has to perform the act of Abbhāna. An assembly must be constituted consisting of not less than 20 duly qualified members. The person concerned must present himself before it, and, after stating all the circumstances of his case, prefer a request for Abbhāna. The request must be preferred three times. Then another Bhikkhu will put a Natti in terms of the request on which Anussāvana will follow, these being repeated three times (the act being of the Natticatuttha class). The Sangha will then signify by its silence that the Bhikkhu has been re-habilitated.

I give below an account of the different forms of disciplinary Sanghakammas :—[39]

(*i*) *Parivāsa and Mānatta*—These are the only two disciplinary measures mentioned in the Pātimokkha which may be inflicted by the Sangha on a Bhikkhu who has been guilty of any of the 13 Sanghādisesa offences. The penalty consists in the imposition of certain disabilities. The two measures are inflicted together in case of non-confession; only Mānatta is inflicted in case of confession. Mānatta must always follow Parivāsa. The broad distinction between the two is that Mānatta continues for a determinate period (6 days), while Parivāsa for an indeterminate period. The following are the rules for the determination of the Parivāsa period :

(*a*) *Apaticchanna*– When the offence is confessed without any delay the Parivāsa period if reduced to nil, that is, the guilty Bhikkhu is sentenced to Mānatta only.

(*b*) *Paticchanna*–When the offence is concealed *willingly* the Parivāsa period extends over as many days from the date of the sentence as the has allowed to elapse without confession. The period, it should be remembered, begins to run after the 6 days of Mānatta. If the concealment is unwilling, the sentence is one of Mānatta only (Cullavagga, III, 23.5).

(*c*) *Suddhanta*–When it is found impossible to determine the date or dates of the commission of an offence or a number of offences or the nature thereof, the Parivāsa period extends over as many days as intervene between the date of the sentence and the date of the ordination of the guilty Bhikkhu.

(*d*) *Samodhāna*–When another offence is committed during the continuance of the Parivāsa period, a fresh period begins to run from the date of the commission of the second offence and extends over as many days as were covered by the Parivāsa period prescribed for the first offence or the Parivasa period prescribed for the second offence, whichever period may be longer.

A general Parivāsa of four months is prescribed for a convert coming from another sect or for a convert who had previously turned renegade. Butthis can hardly be called a disciplinary measure.

(*ii*) *Tajjaniya Kamma*–This measure could be carried out for any transgression whatsoever, except Pārājika and Sanghadisesa offences, even for living 'in lay society, in unlawful association with the world' which is not an offence at all under the Pātimokkha. The penalty consists in the imposition of certain disabilities. These penal disabilities continue for an indeterminate period till the request for Abbhāna is made by the Bhikkhu under sentence and is granted by the Sangha.

(*iii*) *Nissaya Kamma*—This measure could be carried out against a Bhikkhu who had been repeatedly guilty of Sanghādisesa offences and undergone sentences therefore. The penalty consists in subjecting the guilty Bhikkhu to surveillance. The period is as above.

(*iv*) *Pabbājaniya Kamma*—This measure could be carried out against a number of Bhikkhus who by their overt and blamable conduct had created a scandal at a certain place. The penalty consists in banishment from that place. The Sangha which pronounces the sentence of banishment has to proceed in a body to the place where the disciplinary act is to be performed. (Cullavagga, I, 16.1). The period is as above.

(*v*) *Patisāraniya Kamma*—This measure could be carried out against a Bhikkhu who had given offence to a house-holder. The guilty Bhikkhu is enjoined to ask to and obtain pardon of the house-holder whom he has offended. A companion may be appointed by the usual Natti to accompany him. The guilty Bhikkhu must first ask pardon of the offended house-holder. In case he does not obtain pardon, the companion should intercede on his behalf. If he is not pardoned even then, the companion should personally ask the house-holder to pardon the guilty Bhikkhu. If not pardoned even then, the companion should ask pardon for him in the name of the Sangha. If the pardon be not obtained even after that, the companion should make the guilty Bhikkhu confess his guilt in the presence of the offended house-holder in an attitude of humility. The period of sentence is as above.

The counterpart to Patisāraniya-kamma is an act called Patta-nikkujjana (lit. turning down of the begging-bowl). When a Bhikkhu gives offence to a householder, he has to submit to the former penalty; in the converse case the house-holder is subjected to the penalty of having the privilege of giving alms to Bhikkhus and thereby acquiring merit withdrawn.[40]

(*vi*) *Ukkhepaniya Kamma*—This measure could be carried out against a Bhikkhu for three causes, *viz*., (*a*) for not acknowledging a fault, (*b*) for not atoning for a fault, and (*c*) for not renouncing a false or sinful doctrine. The penalty consists in the imposition of certain disabilities. With regard to (*c*), it is laid down that the Bhikkhus should first exhort the guilty Bhikkhu to give up the false doctrine (so that his refusal to do so would amount to Pācittiya, No. 68).[41] Now in Pācittiya, No. 69, it is suggested that a Bhikkhu, guilty of Pācittiya No. 68, should be subjected to a social boycott by the Bhikkhus.[42] The present Sanghakamma is based on this old rule. The sentence in an Ukkhepaniyakamma must be proclaimed against the guilty Bhikkhu in all āvāsas.[43] In case the sentenced Bhikkhu left the Order, the sentence was withdrawn because in that case it became inoperative.[44]

(*vii*) *Pakāsaniya Kamma*—This seems to have been an exceptional measure being referred to only once in the Vinayapitaka, in Cullavagga, VII, 3. 2. It was carried out against Devadatta who without leaving the Order had openly rebelled against it. It consisted in issuing a general proclamation from the Sangha to the effect that it renounced all responsibility for the words and action of the sentenced Bhikkhu. A Bhikkhu was appointed in the usual Natti-form to issue the proclamation.

(*viii*) *Brahmadanda*[45]—This is referred to only once, in the Mahāparinibbāna Sutta, VI, 4. The penalty consists in subjecting the guilty Bhikkhu to a social boycott.[46] No details are given as to what offences would entail this punishment nor as to the manner in which it was to be imposed. It seems to have become obsolete later on, being replaced by other forms of disciplinary Sanghakammas.

An interesting line of investigation is opened up by the question as to how far the Brahmanical Dharmasāstras recognise the laws of the of the Vinayapitaka and what place they assign to these laws. Such an enquiry will help us to understand whether the laws of the Buddhist Sanghas were really of a positive state-enforced character. We have observed that the Bhikkhus were at first a dispersed body of wandering hermits who would naturally have little relation with the political organisation of society. But this could hardly be said of the Bhikkhus of later times—say, a hundred years after the death of Buddha. At that time they constituted a well-organised community, grouped into āvāsas scattered over different parts of the country, each Sangha governed by its monastic laws, owning and possessing property, coming frequently as bodies corporate into legal relations with outsiders, and exercising executive, legislative and judicial functions over each individual member. The communal life of the Bhikkhus thus necessitated the development of a well-organised body of what is known in jurisprudence as *conventional law.*[47] Now there is clear proof in Sanskrit legal literature that conventional law called Samaya, was fully recognised and given effect to by ancient Indian states. The system of Government however which is contemplated in the legal literature of the Hindus is of a purely monarchical type, tempered by constitutional restraints. Our information about the ancient republican states of India, which existed side by side with the monarchies, is meagre in the extreme, but it may be safely presumed that in these states also conventional law was as much respected as in the Hindu monarchies.

In the Arthasāstra of Kautilya it is definitely laid down that it is the duty of a monarch to punish infringements of Samayas or conventional laws (samayavyatikrama). By Samayas, Kautilya means those of Desha, Jāti, Kula and Sangha.[48] In the Sārnath inscription, we find Asoka laying down a penal law for those who seek to bring about schisms in the Buddhist Sangha.[49] In doing so, Asoka only acted in accordance with a well-established principle of the constitution and did not pretend to exercise any authority as the head of the Sangha, as Vincent Smith would have us believe.[50] The idea of the king being the head of the Church, though acceptable to a Protestant Englishman like Vincent Smith, would be quite incomprehensible to an Indian Buddhist of Asoka's time. Similarly Jājnavalkya mentions Sreni, Naigama, Pākhandi and Gana, and says that their old customary laws must be maintained.[51] In the Mitāksarā, Pākhandi is explained as those who do not subscribe to the authority of the Vedas such as the Nagnas (which may refer to the Ājīvakas or the Digambara Jainas), Saugatas (Buddhists), etc.[52] Nārada mentions

Pākhandi, Naigama, Sreni, Pūga, Vrāta and Gana.[53] Manu mentions Grāma, Desha and Sangha.[54] Medhātithi explains Sangha as follows:—

एकधर्म्मानुगतानां नानादेशवासिनां नानाजातीयानामपि प्राणिनां समूहः यथा भिक्षूणांसडधो वणिजां सडाघच्चतुर्व्विदानां सड़घ इति ।

Here the Bhikkhu-sangha is clearly mentioned. It is thus evident that the laws of the Vinayapitaka enjoyed some sort of state-recognition and were to that extent part of the civil law of the land the infringement whereof was punishable by sovereign authority.

It is necessary to bear this fact in mind in order to understand some passages in the conventional laws of Buddhist Sangha. Two illustrations will suffice. In Mahavagga, VI, 39.1, a certain rule is laid down for the settlement of agricultural rights between the Sangha and outsiders. Now this rule would be meaningless and inoperative, if it had not the sanction of the state at its back: an outsider *ipso facto* would not be bound by a rule laid down by the unsupported authority of the Buddhist Sangha. In a Pabbājaniya-kamma again, the Sangha passes a sentence of banishment against a number of Bhikkhus residing in a locality. This sentence would have little terror and no effect if it was not backed by the executive authority of the state. It may be presumed that if a sentence of banishment was passed against a number of Bhikkhus who had made themselves a nuisance at a certain place, they would be compelled by the executive officer of the state to leave the place if a case were brought against them before the king's tribunal. In all cases in fact where there was a chance of the Sangha failing to enforce its decrees, the executive authority of the sovereign power might be invoked. The sovereign under such circumstances would probably act on the instructions of a Vinayadhara for as Jīmūtavāhana says in the Vyavahāra-Mātrikā on the authority of old texts[55]—

येषान्तु समयादेव वहुशोव्यवस्था तेषां समय ज्ञैरेवव्यवहारस्य निर्णयः कर्त्तव्य।

References

1. *Primitive Culture* (1891), Vol. I, p. 20.
2. In the Digha Nikāya; see 17-33.
3. See *Sāmanna-phala Sutta-vannanā.* (See *Sumangala-vilāsini,* P.T.S., pp. 160-165).
4. This is translated in Hoernle's *Uvāsaga-Dasāo* in Bibliotheca Indica Series.
5. See *Bhagavati Sutta* in Bibliotheca Indica Series.
6. See the Cave Dedications of Dasaratha.
7. Jacobi's *Jaina Sutras,* S.B.E., Pt. I, p. 288, footnote 2.
8. *Ibid.*, p. 296.
9. See Oldenberg' *Vinayapitakam*, Vol. III, p. 313.
10. An 'ācariya' in the Vinayapitaka is the instructor of an individual Bhikkhu or a limited number of Bhikkhus. He does not preside over a wide circle of pupils. He stands not in relation to the Sangha, but to individual Bhikkhus whom he watches over. By 'ācariya' in the passage referred to, Buddhaghosa means something quite different from this. Buddhaghosa attributes to the position of an 'ācariya' something of a public character.
11. For an interesting note on Buddhaghosa's native place by the later Prof. Harinath De, see Copleston's *Buddhism, Primitive and Modern,* p. 201, footnote.
12. "The Order of Buddhist presents so long as the Master is alive, a union of teacher and scholars after the Brahmanical model. The transition of such a community, so to speak, from a monarchical type to a republican, its passing somehow, when the teacher dies, into a confederacy of independent members existing side by side, is wholly unknown to the religious systems of the Brahmans. This very transition has completed itself in Buddhism."—Oldenberg's *Buddha* (translated by Hoey, 1882).
13. See II, 24-26.
14. Cited by Oldenberg—See *The Buddha,* p. 341, footnote.
15. Asatam bhāvan iccheyya purekkhāran ca bhikkhusu, *Āvāsesu ca issaryam* pūjā parakulesu ca.—Fausböll's *Dhammapada,* No. 73 (Bāla-vagga).
16. Mahavagga, X, 6.3.
17. For this well-known incident of monastic history, see Maitland's *Dark Ages*, p. 178.
18. See Ch. V of the *Rule of Saint Benedict* (Gasquet's translation). See Gibbon on obedience of the Monks in Ch. XXXVII of *Decline and Fall.* "A blind submission to the commands of the abbot, however absurd or even criminal they might seem, was the ruling principle, the first virtue of the Egyptian monks; and their patience was frequently exercised by the most extravagant trials."—See *Decline and Fall* (The World's Classics), Vol. IV, pp. 77-78.

19. See Cullavagga, VI, 64—"Anujanāmi bhikkave yathāvuddham abhivādanam paccutthānam anjalikammam sāmīcikammam aggāsanam aggodakam aggapindam," and *ibid.*, 13, 2.

20. Rhys Davids says: "The earliest Buddhist records reveal the survival, side by side with more or less powerful monarchies, of republics with either complete or modified independence."—*Buddhist India,* p. 2. See also pp. 19, 22. "Republics are mentioned in various Sanskrit works."—K.P. Jayaswal's *An Introduction to Hindu Polity* (Modern Review, May, 1913, p. 537). See *ibid*, pp. 537-541.

21. *An Introduction to Hindu Polity,* (Modern Review, June, 1913), p. 664.

22. For the rules of Chanda which coincide with the rules of Parisuddhi, see Mahavagga, II, 23-25.

23. Yāvakīvan ca bhikkhave bhikkhū samaggā sannipatissanti samaggā vutthahissanti *samaggā sanghakaranīyāni karissanti* vuddhi yeva bhikkhave bhikkhūnam pātikankhā no parihāni—*Mahāparinibbāna Suttanta,* i, 6.

24. See Mahavagga, IX, 4.2.

25. Mahavagga, IX, 3.2.

26. Observe that the distinction, noticed also by the learned translators, between the six cases given in Mahavagga, IX, 3.7 and those in 3.5 consists in the inversion of the Natti and the Kammavācā. Compare also 3. 9 which sets out all the elements of a valid Sanghakamma.

27. The enumeration is based on Mahavagga, IX, 3.9.... "Nattidutiye ce bhikkhave kamme pathamam nattim thapeti, pacchā ekāya kammavācāya kammam karoti, yāvatikā bhikkhū kammanpattā te āgatā honti, chandārahānam chando āhato hoti, sammukhībhūtā na patikkosanti, dhammena samaggakammam." The same *utatis mutandis* for a Natticatuttha Kamma.

28. Jo pana bhikkhu jānam jathādhammam nihatādhikaranam punakammāva ukkoteyya pācittiyam.

29. The above classification and description of Adhikaranas is based on Cullavagga, IV, 14. The following summary is given by Buddhaghosa in the *Kankhāvittarani:*

    Adhikaranesu tava dhammoti va adhammoti va attarasahi vatthuhi vivadantanam bhikkunam jo vivado idam vivadadhikaranam nama. Silavipattiya va acara-ditthi-ajiva-vipattiya va anuvadantanam jo anuvado upavadana ceva codana ca idam anuvadadhikarana Nama matikaya agata panca vibhange dveti sattapi appatikkhanda apattadhikaranam nama. Jam sanghassa apalokanadinam catunnam kammanam karanam idam kiccadhikaranam nama.

30. As regards these exceptions, compare the rule of Vrihaspati, cited by Jīmūtavahana in the *Vyavahāramātrikā* (edited by Sir A.T. Mookerjee in Memoirs of A.S.B., Vol. III, No. 5, 1912), p. 285:

    गुरुशिष्यौ पित्रापुत्रौ दम्पती स्वामिभृत्यकौ ।
    एतेषां समवेतानां व्यवहारो न सिध्यति ॥

31. An enumeration of them occurs in the last section of the Pātimokkha. They are explained and elaborated with illustrations in Cullavagga, IV, 14.
32. The above account of the Adhikaransamatthas is based on Cullavagga, IV, 14. Every statement made by me here is authorised by some passage or other of the afore-mentioned chapter of Cullavagga. It would be tedious as well as unprofitable to quote all the references.
33. See Cullavagga, XII, 2. 8.
34. The whole passage, which is too long to be given here, is quoted by Oldenberg in *Vinayapitakam,* Vol. II, p. 315.
35. The translation is mine.
36. This is what reason would suggest. But it will be noticed that in the forms of procedure applicable to an Āpattādhikarana, Tassa-papiyyasikā does not occur. One naturally feels diffident in stretching a rule of law by reasoning when one remembers the famous dictum of Lord Halsbury in the case of Quinn *vs*. Leathem about the logical character of the law. Lord Halsbury's dictum is applicable not only to civil law but to canon law as well, for both are historic growths.
37. I am solely responsible for the above chart.
38. This is implied by the expressions occurring in Cullavagga, IV, 4.10, 'āyasmā Dabbo Mallaputto sativepullappatto sangham sativinayam yācati' and āyasmato Dabbassa Mullaputtassa sativepullappattassa sativinayo.'
39. The above account is based on Cullavagga, I-III.
40. Cullavagga, V, 20.6-7.
41. The example of a 'pāpaka ditthi' given in Cullavagga, I, 32.1 is, as the learned translators have pointed out, word for word the same as that given in Pācittiya, 68.
42. Jo pana bhikkhu jānam tathāvādinā (referring to Pāc, 68) bhikkhunā akatānudhammena tam ditthim appatinissatthena saddhim sambhujjeyya vā samva seyya vā saha vā seyyam kappeyya Pācittiyam.
43. See Cullavagga, I, 25 – āvāsaparamparam ca bhikkhave samsatha: Channo bhikkhu āpattiyā adassane ukkhepaniyakammakato asambhogam sanghenā' ti. In the other cases of Ukkhepaniyakamma, the same proclamation is to be made *mutatis mutandis.*
44. See Cullavagga, I, 34. *This withdrawal of the sentence applied only in the case of an Ukkhepaniyakamma for not renouncing a sinful doctrine.*
45. Not mentioned in Cullavagga, I.
46. Channasso Ānanda bhikkhuno mamaccayena brahmadando Kātabbo ti. Katamo pana bhante brahmadando ti. Channo Ānanda bhikkhu yam iccheyya tam vadeyya, so bhikkhūhi n'eva vattabbo na ovaditabbo na anusāsitabbo'ti.
47. "By conventional law is meant any rule or system of rules agreed upon by persons for the regulation of their conduct towards each other. * * * In many cases conventional law is also civil law; for the rules which persons

by mutual agreement lay down for themselves are often enforced by the state."— Salmond's *Jurisprudence* (Fourth Edition), pp. 54-55.

48. तेन देशजातिकुलशङ्घानां समयस्यानपाकर्म्म व्याख्यातम्—

Kautilya's *Arthasastra* (Mysore Government Publication), p. 173.

49. See Smith's *Asoka,* 2nd Ed., p. 195; *cf.*, Kausambi and Sanchi Edicts on the same subject.

50. The penal law laid down in the Sarnath, Kausambi and Sanchi edicts relating to the unfrocking and expulsion of schismatics is based clearly on Mahavagga, I, 67—Sanghabhedako bhikkhave anupasampanno na upasampādetabbo *upasampanno nāsetabbo*. The king only upholds the conventional law of the Buddhist Sanghas an accordance with the immemorial constitutional practice of a Hindu Monarch. But Vincent Smith says of the Sarnath Edict: "This edict exhibits Asoka in his latter years acting as both emperor and Head of the Church. His position, as observed elsewhere, much resembled that of Charlemagne." (Smith's *Asoka*, p. 195, footnote 3). This statement is a remarkable instance of an historian's mental bias perverting his view of history.

51. See Yājnavalkya, II, 192.

52. पाखण्डिनी ये वेदस्य प्रामाण्यमेव नेच्छन्ति नग्राः सौगतादयः

53. See Nārada, Tit. X, 13.

54. See Manu, VIII, 219.

55. See *Vyavahāra Mātrikā*, edited by Sir. A.T. Mukherjee in *Memoirs* of A.S.B., Vol, III, No. 5, p. 281.

7

Communal Life at an Āvāsa

We have observed in Chapter III that if was usual for a person after he had renounced the household for the sake of religious life to seek admittance to a Gana or Sangha of Paribrajakas, acknowledging its leader as his spiritual master (Satthā). The admittance into the Buddhist Sangha was called Upasampadā. Upasampadā might be sought by one who had previously been a Paribrājaka, belonging to a different sect or one who wanted straightway to pass into the Buddhist Sangha from household life.

The earliest formula for admission into the Buddhist Sangha was that of Ehi Bhikkhu[1] which was in all probability the very formula used by Buddha himself—the leader formally inviting candidate for admission to join his Sangha. Afterwards when the dispersed body of Buddha's followers had organised themselves into an Order which acknowledged no one living person as leader, the formula of invitation was changed into one of confession of faith—the Saranāgama. At a later stage when the āvāsas and resident Sanghas had come into being the ordination became an act of the Sangha—a Sanghakamma with all the features of Natti, etc., pertaining thereto.[2] The minimum number competent to perform it was as a general rule laid down as ten.[3] A distinction which did not formerly exist was now drawn between Pabbajjā and Upasampadā.[4] The Upasampadā could not be conferred on a youth of less than twenty and Pabbajjā on a youth of less than fifteen.[5] A candidate for Upasampadā who had previously been of a different religious persuasion (annatitthiyapubbo) had to go through a period of preliminary discipline called Parivāsa extending over four months.[6] Certain exceptions, the significance of which it is difficult for us to understand, were admitted in favour of the Jatilakas and the Sākyas as regards the Parivāsa period.[7] The exception in favour of the latter, it is said, was made by Buddha himself as a concession to his kinsmen.[8] This might have been so. But the exception in favour of the former is said to have been made on the ground that they were Kiriyavādins.[9] Now this ground appears to be rather insufficient. The Kiriyavādins constituted, as we gather from Jaina literature, one of the four schools of philosophy current at that time.[10] It must have included several religious sects and orders besides the Jatilakas. The Jainas, for instance, considered themselves as Kiriyavadins.[11] The ground made out in favour of the Jatilakas can therefore be no valid or sufficient ground for exception. It would rather seem that there was something in the very character of the Jatilakas which entitled them to accept the life of the Buddhist Bhikkhu without passing through a period of probation. The Jatilakas, as their name implies, were a class of persons who wore matted hair which they are said to have shorn off on receiving Upasampadā.[12] They lived outside society, did penances (for which their leader Uruvela was specially renowed),[13] performed sacrifices and kept up the sacred fire.[14] From this description it appears that they were Brahmanical Hindus in the Vānaprastha or Tāpasa stage of life.[15] Now according to the Brahmanical rule, the fourth stage of Paribrajaka comes immediately after the third stage of Vānaprastha, and the conjecture may be hazarded that the exemption of the Parivāsa period in favour of the Jatilakas was a concession to the Brahmanical rule according to which a person who had gone through the penances of the Vānaprastha stage was entitled to embrace at once the life of the religious mendicant. But the conjecture is put forward with some diffidence.

When a person had been admitted into the Sangha by the formal Kammavācā, he became a member thereof with full rights and privileges. As I have said in the previous chapter, the constitution of a Buddhist Sangha was perfectly democratic and as regards constitutional rights and privileges all were on the same footing. But it was usual for a newly-admitted member to live in Nissaya or spiritual tutelage with a senor of at least ten years' standing called Upajjhāya or Ācariya.[16] The rules of Nissaya however were not at all hard and fast. The usual period was ten years. But it is said that a learned competent Bhikkhu might live in Nissaya for five years only, while an unlearned one all his life.[17] Nissaya was remitted in several exceptional cases.[18] The Nissaya rules regulating conduct between a Upajjhaya (he was the person formally chosen by the neophyte as his instructor at the Ordination) and Saddhīviharika and an Ācariya and Antevāsika are an exact replica of the Brahmacarya rules of the Hindus.[19] The very word Brahmacarya is used to describe the condition of a Bhikkhu who lives in Nissaya. It also appears that the Acariya was the actual instructor and the Upajjhāya who was formally elected at the Upasampadā was instructor only in name. The latter however enjoyed a higher status, for it is said that when the Upajjhāya and Ācariya come together, nissaya towards the catter ceases.[20] There was however absolutely no difference between the duties and obligations of an Ācariya and those of a Upajjhāya.[21]

When a Bhikkhu was duly ordained, he became member of a Sangha resident at an Āvāsa. The Āvāsa was a colony of Buddhist Bhikkhus, consisting of many Vihāras, located generally in an Ārāma or park donated by some wealthy lay-devotee.[22] The ārāma was fenced round, having a bathing tank at the entrance.[23] Inside this enclosure, scattered over the whole park, were rectangular buildings (Vihāras) with many cells (Parivenas) for the Bhikkhus to live in. The cells were provided with casements.[24] Inside each cell the furniture was of the simplest kind fitted to the simple needs and small comforts of a homeless religieux. The floor was spread at night with a cover (Bhummattharana) which was rolled up in the morning. There was a bedstead resting on movable supporters (Mancapatipādakā) which were put aside in the morning. The bed consisted of a mattress, a mat and a pillow. By the side of it, stood a spittoon (Khelamallaka). A board against which the Bhikkhu could recline (Apassenaphalaka) and a seat (Pītha), probably resting on jointed legs (for it is said—pītham nīcam katvā, turning down the seat), completed the furniture.[25] The alms-bowl, the clothes, the tooth-brush and a few other most necessary articles made up the whole personal belongings of a Bhikkhu.

Though the vihāras stood separately all over the ārāma, all property was joint and intended for the common use of the whole ārāma. There were a storeroom (Kotthaka), a refectory (Upatthānasālā), a fire-room or kitchen (Aggisālā), a warehouse (Kappiyakutī), a privy (Vaccakutī), a common room (Cankama), an arcade for walking exercises (Cankamanasālā), a common bath (Jantāghara), bath-rooms (Jantāgharasālā), a pavilion (Mandapa) probably for holding assemblies in, and a well (Udapāna), walled round and covered (Udapāna-sālā).[26] The right of property in these things was vested in the corporate body and not in any individual.

On the decease of a Bhikkhu, the succession to all the property which had been appropriated by him for personal use was governed by the following law: the Sangha became owner (sāmi) of his bowl and robes; but these were usually assigned by the Sangha to those who had waited upon the Bhikkhu in his last illness perhaps as a sort of perquisite; small utensils and light furniture (lahubhandam lahuparikkhāram) were divided among members of the Sangha present there, but heavy utensils and heavy furniture (garubhandam garuparikkhāram) were not to be thus apportioned and distributed, for they belonged not to the particular Sangha of which the deceased was a member, but to the whole Bhikkhu community present or future (āgatānāgatassa cātuddisassa sanghassa).[27]

The most important part of the Sangha-property was the Kappiyakutī in which provisions for the whole Sangha were stored. The institution of it has a curious history which betrays the gradual modification of eremitical life which we have already described. When the Bhikkhus were a dispersed body of wandering mendicants, there could be no question of the joint storage of provisions. Pācittiyas 35 and 38, which lay down the original rule of mendicancy exclude the storage of provisions—the first rule being that the given quantity of food must be consumed at one meal (although things left over might be taken).[28] These rules are amplified and emphasised in Mahavagga, VI, 17.1-6. At a time of scarcity at Rajagaha, it is said, the rules were relaxed for a time (*ibid.*, 7), but were reinforced as soon as the necessity was over (*ibid.*, VI, 32-2). When, however, cenobitical societies grew up and the Bhikkhus began to live at āvāsas in collective bodies, it became necessary to keep up storage of food. But this could not be done without contravening the old rule of mendicancy that had been inherited from the individualistic and eremitical stage which the Sangha had completely out-grown in later times. The difficulty was got round by a legal fiction, by assigning for storage of provisions (Kappiyabhumi) a vihāra lying *out-side* (paccantima vihāra—Mahavagga, VI, 33.2). It had to be fixed by the usual Natti. If not, the store might be kept in an ox-stall (gonisādika) or in a lay man's premises (Mahavagga, VI, 33.4). Drugs might be kept in any duly appointed place besides these (*ibid.*, 5). The place was in charge of an officer called Kappiyakāraka the most important of whose functions was to determine what provisions were allowable and what not;[29] and a lay man wishing to give money to the Sangha had to make it over to the Kappiyakāraka to be converted into suitable provisions.[30]

According to Pācittiya, 82, property given to the Sangha could not be appropriated by an individual.[31] An individual thus might claim the right of user, but not the right of property in anything. If a person wished to make a gift, even of food, to an individual Bhikkhu, he had to send it to the Sangha saying, "This is to be given to the Sangha with special reference to so-and-so" (*cf.* ayyassa Upanandassa dassetvā sanghassa dātabban ti—Mahavagga, VI, 19.1).[32] This idea of communal ownership of property is emphasised in the Mahāparinibbāba Suttanta, I, 11, where it is said: "Yāvakīvan ca bhikkhave bhikkhū ye te lābhā dhammikā dhammaladdhā antamaso pattapariyāpanna-mattam pi tathārupehi tābhehi appativi bhattabhojī bhavissanti sīlavanteḥi sabrahmacārīhi sādhārana-bhogī vuddhi yeva bhikkhave bhikkhūnam patikankhā no parihāni." The reader will remember an exactly similar rule which obtained in medieval Christian monasteries.[33] The old rule is more definitely laid down in Cullavagga, VI, 15.2 and 16.2, where the following five descriptions of things are said to be non-transferable and non-apportionable, *viz.*, (*a*) Ārāma or its site, (*b*) Vihāra or its site, (*c*) Bed, chair, bolster and pillow, (*d*) Brass vessel, brass jar, brass pot, brass vase, razor, axe, hatchet, hoe and spade, and (*e*) creepers, bamboos, *Munja* or *Babbaja* grass, common grass, clay, wooden things and crockery. Now suppose a number of Bhikkhus built a vihāra for themselves. It would not thereby become the property of those Bhikkhus, but of the whole Sangha and any Bhikkhu coming there might claim a Senāsana (seat) as of right. On this principle that a vihāra was always a *sanghika vihāra,* the notorious six Bhikkhus sought to oust a number of Bhikkhus who had built a vihāra for themselves by their own labour.[34] It was laid down, following the same principle on this occasion, that the in-coming Bhikkhus must not turn out the Bhikkhus already in possession of the vihāra. This illustration is taken in Cullavagga, VI, 11.1. Difficulties would sometimes arise about agricultural rights between the Sangha which was a body corporate and out-siders. A rule for the determination of such rights is laid down in Mahavagga, VI, 39.1. If seedlings belonging to outsiders grew up on the grounds of the Sangha, the Sangha might appropriate the crops after giving a part (Buddhaghosa makes it 1/12)[35] to the other. If one the other hand seedlings belonging to the Sangha grew up on the grounds of an out-sider, the Sangha might likewise take the crops after giving the same portion to the out-sider.

For the conduct of the multifarious business of the Sangha, there existed several officers in an āvāsa, all appointed by the usual Natti. The following is a classified list of Sangha Officers:—

(A) Connected with commissariat[36] –

(*i*) Bhandāgārika—Overseer of stores.

(*ii*) Kappiyakāraka—It was the duty of this officer to ascertain what provisions were allowable and what not. He would receive gifts of money from laymen and convert them into proper commodities.

(*iii*) Sanghabhatta—Apportioner of rations. His function was to dole out rations by ticketing each person's share.

(*iv*) Cīvabhājaka—Distributor of congey.

(*v*) Yāgubhājaka—Distributor of Yāgu (a kind of rice-pulp).

(*vi*) Phalabhājaka—Distributor of fruits.

(*vii*) Khajjakabhājaka—Distributor of dry food (what the Bengalis call Khājā).

(B) Connected with chambers, wardrobe, etc.[37]—

(*viii*) Senāsana-pannāpaka—Chamberlain. His business was to arrange seats for the Bhikkhus. The seats were arranged three times a year, *viz.*, on the day of the commencement of earlier Vassa, on the day of commencement of later Vassa, and on the day after the Pavāranā.

(*ix*) Cīvarapatiggāhaka—Receiver of robes. Laymen used to make gifts of robes to the Sangha, specially at the close of the vassa which it was the business of this officer to receive.

(*x*) Sātiyagāhāpaka—Distributor of under-garments.

(*xi*) Pattagāhāpaka—Distributor of alms-bowls.

(*xii*) Appamattaka-vissajjaka—Disposer of trifles. His business was to distribute among the members of the Sangha such small articles as needles, scissors, sandals, girdles, butter, honey, etc., according to their wants.[38]

(C) Superintendents—

(*xiii*) Navakammika—Superintendent of new buildings.

(*xiv*) Ārāmikapesaka—Overseer of the Ārāmikas. The Ārāmīka was a servant employed by the donor of an Ārāma to keep the grounds in order. This officer's business was to supervise the work of such servants.

(*xv*) Samanerapesaka—Superintendent of the Samaneras. His function was to look after the novices who had not yet obtained Upasampadā.

The above with the exception perhaps of the Navakammika were permanent officers. Temporary officers, like the Kanthina-vitthāraka. Salāka-gāhāpaka, etc., might be appointed for any purpose. Designations of other officers also occur elsewhere than in the Vinayapitaka, *e.g.*[39]

(*xvi*) Paniyavārika—Officer in charge of drinks.

(*xvii*) Bhajanavārika—Officer in charge of utensils.

(*xviii*) Upadhivāra—Probably a Steward.

(*xix*) Parisandavārika—Officer in charge of the groves.

(*xx*) Mundasayanāsana-vārika—Officer in charge of lodgings temporarily not is use.

The āvāsas, as we have already remarked, were primarily intended for the customary rain-retreat, which was brought to a close by two characterisitic ceremonies, *viz.*, Pavāranā and Kanthina. The Pavāranā[40] was a solemn conference at which each Bhikkhu requested the assembly to call him to account if they had seen or heard or suspected him to be guilty of any transgression during the period of Vassa. The 'invitation' was made in a set, elliptical formula[41] though it had no practical significance at all, because the matter one was to be charged with had to be previously brought to an issue just as in Parisuddi before Uposatha. For minor offences, this would be done in the following way: A for example was aware that B had committed an offence. A would ask leave of B to reprove him for the offence.[42] If B gave leave and A reproved him accordingly, he was entitled to join the Pavāranā. But omission of this preliminary step would entail inhibition of the Pavāranā by formal resolution for the guilty Bhikkhu. For major offences, *viz.*, Pārājika, Sanghādisesa, Thullaccaya, Pācittiya, Pātidesaniya, Dukkata and Dubbāsita, of which the guilty Bhikkhu stood confessed, mere friendly reproof would not suffice. The guilty Bhikkhu must first be dealt with according to law. In case of a doubt as to the nature of the offence, the Bhikkhu should be dealt with for the lighter offence.[43] The inhibition of the Pavāranā however was hedged in with strict conditions. Only an intelligent Bhikkhu of pure character was entitled to inhibit the Pavāranā of a Bhikkhu.[44] And then he was liable to be sharply cross-examined by the assembly with regard to the charge that he brought forward,[45] and if the cross-examination disclosed a false or mistaken charge, the Bhikkhu who wanted to inhibit another's Pavāranā was himself subjected to legal proceedings for bringing a false or mistaken charge.[46] The Pavāranā ceremony might be postponed (Pavāranā samgaha) till the next Komudi Cātumāsi day if the Bhikkhus at an āvāsa wanted to prolong their Vassa residence.[47]

The Kanthina[48] was the ceremony of the distribution of robes. The details of this ceremony are rather obscure and confusing and would be tedious to recount. But the general features are clear enough. Each Sangha possessed a store of robes (Kanthina-dussa). This consisted of raw cotton, cloth or rags.[49] An officer was appointed by the usual Natti to whom this store was made over before the Kanthina ceremony. He caused suitable robes to be made out of it. When the new robes had been prepared, he performed a symbolical act, called Atthāra (spreading), putting aside his own old robe and spreading out a new one for himself in its place. After this, he specified which of the robes were suitable for the Theras (older members) and which for the Navakas (younger members). Then the Sangha tacitly ratified the act. It was now time 'when each of the Bhikkhus could transmute his claim to an undivided share into the actual possession of a divided share.'[50] This claim which it was not necessary to enforce immediately, continued to subsist on two conditions (Palibodha), *viz.*, Āvāsa (the Bhikkhu's domicile) and Cīvara (the condition of his clothes). There was no need for immediately taking possession of a robe, if these conditions were satisfied, that is, if the Bhikkhu did not leave the āvāsa and if his clothes were really worn out and he stood in need of a new set of robes, he could get one within the prescribed time after the ceremony of Atthāra. Meantime the Bhikkhu might get a new robe as a gift from a lay man or his old robe might not have got quite worn out. During the period that the Kanthina robe was not appropriated by a Bhikkhu, certain privileges were granted to him chiefly with a view to enabling him to satisfy his needs from other sources. If however he found that there was no chance for it, he proceeded to participate in the store of robes with the formal permission of (perhaps) the Kanthina-vitthāraka.[51]

In the last chapter we have given an account of the communistic and republican government of a Buddhist Āvāsa. This government was in its truest sense 'Government by discussion.' There was no superimposed authority to act as a clog on the utmost freedom of discussion, and it is curious to observe how in many cases the standard of the rightness of any proposal is said to be the Dhamma. We who have drifted far from the mentality of our forefathers of so many centuries ago shall probably never be able to realise the full significance of this term. But one thing is clear, *viz.*, that the standard of Dhamma was not an objective but a subjective one.[52] In the Mahāparinibbāna Sutta, Buddha calls upon the Bhikkhus to be 'atta-dīpā atta-saranā dhamma-dīpā dhamma saranā,' which gives us the key-note to the aggressive individualism of life at a Buddhist āvāsa with which no reader of the Vinayapitaka can fail to be struck. Where everybody had full right to think for himself and to publish his thoughts, differences of opinion could not but arise. In Cullavagga, VII, 5.2, it is said that a schism (Sanghabheda) could arise on any of the eighteen matters which may be summarised as relating to (*i*) Dhamma (1-2), (*ii*) Vinaya (3-4), (*iii*) Teachings, practices and ordainments of the Tathāgata (5-10), (*iv*) Offences and rules relating to them (11-18). The same points substantially are mentioned in Cullavagga, IV, 14.2, as giving rise to Vivādādhikarana. It is important to note the distinction between the two. In a Vivādādhikarana the difference was honest and was not intended to bring about a permanent cleavage. It was duly placed before the Sangha and decided by voting and after the decision it was not to be reopened on penalty of a Pācittiya. But such a difference might also be dishonest or intentional, brought about on purpose to cause a schism. There was no power except the terror of curses invoked in Cullavagga, VII, 5.5 (and the terror of expulsion by the king—*vide* Asoka's Sarnath Pillar edict) which could check a dishonest difference when there was no outside standard to which it could be referred. This the Vivāda or ground of difference might be put forward *dishonestly* with knowledge of its falsity or dubious character *together with* an intention to cause a division,[53] or *honestly*, with belief of its rightness, its accordance with Dhamma, *together with* intention to cause a division believed to be right and proper.[54] In both cases intention to bring about a schism is essential which is absent in an ordinary Vivāda which would lead to a Vivādādhikarana. It is clear that a Vivāda which was intentional could not be set at rest by a Vivādādhikarana, and its result would inevitably be a Sanghabheda,—just as the doctrines put forward by the Vijjians were not set at rest by the decision of the Ubbāhikā at Vesali, as we are told by the author of the Dīpawamsa.[55]

When a Sanghabheda did actually take place, the original Sangha was split up into two Sanghas, holding Kammavācā, Uposatha and Pavāranā separately.[56] It was at first considered allowable for them to live within the limits of the same āvāsa,[57] but this was afterwards negatived.[58] The schismatic parties might subsequently coalesce performing a Sāmaggi-uposatha.[59] But in such a case, the ground of difference must entirely disappear and must not be merely covered up. (The *Sangha-sāmaggi* or reunion, as is said in Mahavagga, X, 6.2, might be 'atthāpeta,' in spirit, or 'vyanjanupeta,' in letter only. It was only when the reunion was both in spirit and in letter that it was a true reunion—*Ibid.*) Schisms gave rise to some of the Buddhist sects the earliest of which was the Mahāsanghika.

There were however certain safe-guards against a Sanghabheda. A schism could be brought about (*i.e.*, the Vivāda could be brought to an issue) only by a member of the Sangha who was *Pakatatta* (under no disability), *Samanasamvāsaka* (belonging to the same community) and *Samānasimāya thita* (residing within the same boundary).[60] The Vivāda must be formally placed before an assembly which must not consist of less than nine members—four on one side and four on another side *plus* the Salāka-gāhāpaka.[61] (It will be remembered that Jebhuyyasikā was applicable to a Vivādādhikarana). When the Vivāda was considered by an assembly consisting of less number, it could give rise only to what was called Sangha-rāji (disunion), but not Sangha-bheda (schism).[62] The effect of all the rules is that in order to produce a schism, four competent Bhikkhus must come forward and place a disputed point before an assembly of nine with purpose prepense to cause a division, either knowing that the point was wrong or doubtful (Cullavagga, VII, 5.5) or believing it without due deliberation to be right (*ibid.*, 5.6), and knowing also that schism would result from their action—a schism which to their belief was either wrong, as in the first case, or right as in the second. In all cases, it will be observed, there must be an intention to bring about a schism and this, as we have pointed out, differentiates a Sanghabheda from an ordinary Vivādādhikarana. Let us take two concrete examples: Four Bhikkhus at an āvāsa might say: "Well, this is a point of doctrine which we believe to be right. We shall place it before an assembly. If it is ratified, well and good. If not, we must secede"; or they might say: "Well, etc., etc. If not, we shall as in duty bound acquiesce." In the former case there would arise a Sanghabheda, in the latter case a mere Vivādādhikarana. It will be observed from Cullavagga, VII, 5.6, that if one took up the first attitude he was not liable to condemnation. The intention to produce a schism was not condemnable *per se*. There are surely certain beliefs regarding which a conscientious man would admit no compromise and nobody would hold such a person blameworthy for seceding from a society that did not approve of his faith. Those who are obsessed with the parallelism between monastic communities of the west and those of the east will do well to remember that in the ancient Buddhist Sangha at any rate, the liberty which the organ-voiced author of the *Areopagitica* proclaimed to be 'above all other liberties, *viz.*, to know, to utter, and to argue freely according to conscience,' was guarded with a strict jealousy which would appear strange and almost shocking to medieval Christian monasteries. But this feature of ancient Buddhist monastic life was of a piece with that unfettered freedom of thought in ancient India which was the 'grand invention,' not surely of the Greeks, as European historians aver,[63] but of the Indians long before the Greeks.

References

1. Ehi bhikkhū svākkhāto dhammo caratha brahmacariyam sammā dukkhassa antakiriyāyā ti. It is said in Mahavagga, I. 12, that Saranāgama was substituted for it because the Bhikkhus wanted to confer Pabbajjā and Upasampadā. The distinction between the earlier and the later formulæ is interesting. In the one case the formula is uttered by the person who ordains which is always Buddha himself; in the other case by the person who is ordained. The one is an invitation, the other is a confession of faith. An invitation could be made only by the leader of the Sangha, and, as we have seen, after the death of Buddha, the Buddhist Sangha had never a recognised leader.
2. *Cf.*, Mahavagga I, 12, 28 *et seq.*, 36 *et. seq.*, 76. The ordination ceremony of the Buddhists remains substantially the same as it was in the earliest days.
3. In Mahavagga V, 13.5, Sona is enjoined by Mahakaccayana to obtain Buddha's permission to relax this rule in favour of the inhabitants of the Southern Country and Avanti. The permission was obtained and for those localities the minimum of four Bhikkhus and a Vinayadhara was prescribed.
4. Kern says: "The broad distinction between the first admission, Pravrajyā, and the Ordination, Upasampadā, is clear enough, but if we descend into details, the matter becomes embarrassing."—*Manual of Indian Buddhism,* p. 77. Later on he says: "The passages and testimonies adduced seem to warrant the conclusion that the real ordination or consecration takes place by the Upasampadā, whereas Pravrajyā is the act by which the candidate formally declares his intention to take the vows."—p. 78. Kern seems to think that the distinction had existed from the beginning, but it is not so. I will be observed from the opening sections of Mahavagga, up to I, 24. 4 that all who are ordained under Ehi Bhikkhu Upasampadā ask for Pabbajjā and Upasampadā and get the Upasampadā at once, and not Pabbajjā first, Upasampadā afterwards as was the custom later on.
5. Mahavagga, I, 50; I, 49.6.
6. Mahavagga, I, 38.1.
7. Mahavagga, I, 38.11. The translators render 'aggikā jatilakā' as 'fire-worshippers and Jatilas' which is misleading. It should be 'fire-worshipping Jatilakas,' as the Pali expression clearly refers to one class of men only and not so two classes. Such also seems to be the view of Kern when he speaks of only two classes of persons, etc.,...*Manual of Indian Buddhism,* p. 78.
8. 'Imāham bhikkhave nātīnam āveniyam parihāram dammīti.'
9. 'Kammavādino ete bhikkhave kiriyavādino.'
10. "Jainas enumerate four principal schools of philosophy—Kriyāvāda, Akriyāvāda, Ajnānavāda and Vainayikavāda"—Jacobi's *Jaina Sutras,* S.B.E. Pt. II, Intro. xxvi. The Ājīvakas, as thier doctrines clearly testify, were Akriyāvāda. The Buddhists were often misconstrued as belonging to the same school, *e.g.*, Mahavagga, VI, 34.12 and also 31.5.

11. "It is evident that the Jainas considered themselves Kiriyavādins."—Jacobi's *Jaina Sutras,* Pt. II, p. 319, footnote 2.
12. Mahavagga, I, 20.19.
13. *Ibid.*, 22.4
14. *Ibid.*, 15.2; 19.1; 20.19.
15. Rhys Davids and Oldenberg regard the Jatilakas as Brahmanical Vanaprasthas—See *Vinaya Texts,* S.B.E., Pt. I, p. 118, footnote 1.
16. Mahavagga, I, 32.1.
17. *Ibid.*, 53.4.
18. *Ibid.*, 72.
19. *Ibid.*, 1, 32 and 33=Cullavagga, VIII, 13.4 and Mahavagga, I, 25 and 26=Cullavagga, VIII, 11.12.
20. Mahavagga, I, 36.1 at the end.
21. See *Vinaya Texts*, Pt. I, p. 178, Footnote 2.
22. See Mahavagga, VI, 23.1.
23. Cullavagga, V, 17.1.
24. See Mahavagga, I, 25.15 (where one of the duties of a pupil is said to be rubbing the casement and corners of the master's vihāra—āloka-sandhikannabhāgā pamajjitabbā); 63.3 (where the window is called 'vātāpana'). Also Mahavagga, I, 25.18 (where the pupil must shut or open the windows for the convenience of the master), Cullavagga, VI, 2.2.
25. For the mention of these articles of furniture, see the list of the duties of a pupil in Mahavagga, I, 25.15-16. See also Cullavagga, VI, 2.3, *et. seq.*
26. These adjuncts are mentioned in Mahavagga, III, 5.6 and also in Cullavagga, VI, 4.10 in the description of the Vihāra built by Anathapindada in Jetavana.
27. Mahavagga, VIII, 27.5.
28. Jo pana bhikkhu sannidhikārakam khādanīyam vā bhojanīyam vā khādeyya vā bhunjeyya vā Pācittiyam—No. 38. Jo pana bhikkhu bhuttāvi pavārito anatirittam (translated as 'not left over') khādaniyam vā bhojanīyarn vā khādeyya vā bhunjeyya vā Pācittiyam—No. 35.
29. See Mahavagga, VI, 17.8.
30. See *ibid.*, VI, 34.21.
31. Jo pana bhikkhu jānam sanghikam lābham parinatam puggalassa parināmeyya pācittiyam.
32. This does not apply to gift of Cīvara, perhaps because it was included, in a Bhikkhu's personal belongings.
33. "The candidate who aspired to the virtue of evangelical poverty abjured, at his first entrance into a regular community, the idea, and even the name, of all separate and exclusive possession"—Gibbon's *Decline and Fall,* Ch. XXXVII.

34. Nanu āvuse sanghiko vihāre'ti. āmāvuso sanghiko viharo ti. Utthethāvuso, amhākam vihāre pāpunātīti.

35. This is clearly iniquitous Buddhghosa says it is in accordance with the ancient custom of India. What he means is far from clear. The translators render, bhāgam, as 'half'.

36. All these, except (*ii*), are mentioned in Cullavagga, VI, 21.1.2.

37. Nos. (*viii*) and (*ix*) are mentioned in Cullavagga, VI, 21.2. The rest in Cullavagga, VI, 21.3.

38. Nos. (*xiv*) and (*xv*) are mentioned in Cullavagga, (VI), 21.3.

No. (*xiii*) is mentioned in (VI), 5.2 and elsewhere.

39. See Kern's *Manual of Indian Buddhism,* p. 83.

40. The above account of Pavārana is based on Mahavagga, IV.

41. Sangham āvuso pavāremi ditthena vā sutena vā parisankāya vā, etc.,—Mahavagga, IV, 1.14.

42. Asking leave of a Bhikkhu before reproving him for an offence was in accordance with a rule laid down in Mahavagga, II, 16.1.

43. Mahavagga, IV, 19-22.

44. *Ibid.*, 16 6-9.

45. *Ibid.*, 10-15.

46. *Ibid.*, 16-17.

47. *Ibid.*, 18.1.6

48. The above account of the Kanthina is based on Mahavagga, VII and the illuminating notes of Rhys Davids and Oldenberg on the Chapter in *Vinaya Texts,* Pt. II.

49. Not raw cotton merely—See *Vinaya Texts,* Pt. II, p. 151, footnote 4 and Mahavagga, VII, 1.6.

50. *Vinaya Texts,* Pt. II, p. 152, footnote 1.

51. See *ibid.*, footnote 2.

52. An entire thesis may be written on the significance of this all-important word, Dhamma, in Indian literature, and it is absurd to attempt to dispose of it in a footnote. Its sense too is so kaleidoscopic that it is extremely difficult to fit it.

Observe for instance the use of the word Dhamma in Mahavagtga, X, 5.8 Two Bhikkhus contend over some point of doctrine; how is an outsider to judge? Buddha says: Ubhayatha dhammam sutvā ye tattha dhammavādino tesam ditthin ca khantin ca rucin ca ādāyan ca rocehi, etc. The outsider must judge according to his own subjective standard. The Salākagāhāpaka may reject the voting if it goes against the Dhamma in a case where two parties contend over some point of doctrine. Here also we have a subjective standard recognised. Compare also the use of the word in Cullavagga, IV, 2-3; 14.2 (where some Bhikkshus say, 'This is Dhamma,' while others say, 'This is not Dhamma') and elsewhere. The meaning of Dhamma in every passage where it occurs must be settled relatively to the context and import of the whole passage.

53. This is the case contemplated in Cullavagga, VII, 5.5.
54. This is the case contemplated in Cullavagga, VII, 5.6.
55. *Dipaw.*, V.
56. Cullavagga, VII, 5.2.
57. Mahavagga, X, 1.9.
58. Cullavagga, XII, 2.1 (āvāsakappo).
59. Mahavagga, II, 36.4 and X, 5.14.
60. Cullavagga, VII, 5.1 at the end.
61. Cullavagga, VII, 5.1.
62. *Ibid.*
63. "Freedom of thought was their (*i.e.*, of the Greeks) grand invention"—Sanderson's *History of Greece and Rome,* p. 86.